KEEPING GOD IN
THE SMALL STUFF

Devotions for Every Day

KEEPING GOD IN
THE SMALL STUFF

Devotions for Every Day

Bruce & Stan

PROMISE
PRESS
An Imprint of Barbour Publishing

Published by Promise Press, an imprint of Barbour Publishing, Inc., P.O. Box 719, Uhrichsville, Ohio 44683, http://www.barbourbooks.com

Member of the
Evangelical Christian
Publishers Association

Printed in the United States of America.

INTRODUCTION

If you're like us (and you probably are), you have no difficulty sensing God's presence in the big events of your life. You know that He is with you when the big things happen: births, deaths, marriages, car accidents, losing a job, getting a new job—you get the idea.

But the extraordinary things are infrequent. They happen only once in a while (that's what makes them extraordinary). If we are conscious of God only when the big things happen, then we won't be thinking about Him very much.

God is constantly present and involved in your life. If you want to find Him on a *daily* basis, then you'll need to start looking for Him in the small stuff. The circumstances, relationships, and activities of your normal, everyday routine are where you can find God. He is there—in the commonplace situations of your life.

We have written several books that focus on the theme of God's involvement in the small stuff of life. Not surprisingly, the titles are:

God Is in the Small Stuff and it all matters
God Is in the Small Stuff for Your Family
God Is in the Small Stuff for Your Marriage

These books contain essays about the ordinary issues of life. The response from our readers has been overwhelming. In letters and E-mails that we have received, they confirmed what we know to be true: When you look for God in your life, even the ordinary things become extraordinary.

This book is designed to give you a devotional thought for each day of the year. (As you might expect, it starts with January 1, but don't feel obligated to wait until then to get started.) Start right away to connect with God. He's easy to find. Just look for Him in the small stuff of your life.

Bruce & Stan

GOD IS IN THE SMALL STUFF

Little is much if God is in it.

A national best-selling book suggests that you shouldn't sweat the small stuff. Many people treat the small stuff in life as if no one—not even God—has any control over what happens. They call it "fate" or talk about how they are "lucky" or "fortunate" when certain things happen or don't happen.

We're not suggesting that you should involve God in every decision you make no matter how small (for example, you don't have to ask God what you should wear in the morning). But if you're like most people, you tend to ask for God's involvement only in times of major need or crisis, and consequently you miss out on the joy and wonder of watching God work in the small stuff of your life. There's no question God is in the big events, but He delights in working in the details.

Do not despise these small beginnings,
for the LORD rejoices to see the work begin. . .
ZECHARIAH 4:10

USE FOR THE PURPOSE INTENDED

For your wordsgiveand this Bible has given
to bringthe heart in this

You would laugh if someone expressed belief in a "lucky" rabbit's foot dangling from his key chain. (Okay, maybe you wouldn't laugh, but we are pretty sure that you would snicker.) Why? Because "good luck charms" are foolishness and offer nothing but a false sense of security.

Sadly, some of us relegate our Bible to the status of "good luck charm." Somehow we get a warm, fuzzy feeling just knowing that it is propped up in the bookshelf or lying on the nightstand. But we never read it. It is just there for looks (and for luck).

But the Bible will do you absolutely no good sitting unread. Only if it is opened, read, and studied can you access all of God's wisdom and direction that the Bible contains. You need to know all that God has written for you to learn about Him (and yourself). You need to read the Bible. Move it off the shelf and into your heart.

For these commands and this teaching are
a lamp to light the way ahead of you.
PROVERBS 6:23

In the Beginning

Either God created the heavens and the earth, or He didn't.

Unless we know where our world came from, we don't really know where it's going. And we don't know where we're going, either. That's why there's such a huge debate about how the universe began. The answer goes to the heart of our very existence.

There are only two options when it comes to the beginning of the universe. The first option is that a personal, intelligent, all-powerful, all-knowing, self-existent Creator made the heavens and the earth in perfect balance and harmony. The second option is that everything in the universe came from nothing. It "made" itself. (To get a sense of this, next time you get into your car, imagine that it came into existence on its own without the help of a designer and manufacturer.)

There are no third or fourth options that some impersonal "force" brought the universe into existence, or that a speck of energy exploded into stars and planets and life. Either God made everything or He didn't.

In the beginning God created the heavens and the earth.
GENESIS 1:1 NIV

CONDUCT

*Sometimes you have to choose between following God
and impressing your friends.*

Living a godly life may make you different. You may
end up doing just the opposite of everyone else. Sometimes
you may find that your conduct pleases God but offends your
friends, or vice versa. Should you compromise and try to find
an acceptable middle ground?

Jesus gave the two analogies of "salt" and "light" to
show the importance of conduct. Salt is a seasoning, but it's
also used as a preservative. God wants you to be like a moral
preservative, bringing a virtuous and ethical flavor to your culture. God also wants you to shine into the darkness, not for
your own publicity, but to bring credit to God.

Salt doesn't do any good if it stays in the shaker. A can-
dle doesn't do any good under a bowl. So go forward today being salt and light in your world.

*"You are the light of the world. . .
Don't hide your light under a basket!
. . .let your good deeds shine out for all to see,
so that everyone will praise your heavenly Father."*
MATTHEW 5:14–16

YOU CAN'T PROVE GOD EXISTS

Don't worry about proving God's existence,
because no one can disprove it.

Sometimes we think we can prove God exists, but it just can't be done. You can't stick God under a microscope or view Him through a telescope, because God is a Spirit. No one has actually seen God (John 1:18).

On the other hand, no one can disprove God's existence. If someone says that God doesn't exist because you can't prove it in a science experiment, then you must also conclude that light doesn't exist, because you can't prove that, either.

But light does exist, because there's evidence. We can see it, feel it, and witness the effect of light on the world and in our lives. The same goes for God. We know He exists because we can see the perfect order of the universe. We can feel His presence in our hearts. And we see the evidence of God's involvement in the world and in every detail of our lives.

They can clearly see his invisible qualities—
his eternal power and divine nature.
ROMANS 1:20

WHAT IT TAKES

As you seek to do tasks that are excellent, diligence is required.

The coach of any athletic team will tell you that you've got to practice if you want to win. In the spiritual realm, "winning" is getting to know God and having our lives transformed in the process. But just as in sports, "winning" with God requires the discipline of repeated practice.

As you are diligent in pursuing God, you'll notice gradual changes in your life. Everything won't change all at once. But don't let that discourage you. (God isn't discouraged by it. He won't cut you from the team.) Keep at it. You are working for a goal that is worthy of your best efforts.

*I keep working toward that day when I will finally
be all that Christ Jesus saved me for and wants me to be. . . .
I strain to reach the end of the race
and receive the prize for which God,
through Christ Jesus, is calling us up to heaven.*
PHILIPPIANS 3:12, 14

THERE'S NOTHING YOU CAN DO

Thank God that your salvation does not depend on you.

In the physical world there are many ways to be saved, but first you have to be in a situation where you would eventually die without help. A guy in a lifeboat could pull you out of freezing water, or a skilled surgeon could save your life on the operating table. In either case you would be saved, and there would be nothing you could do to save yourself.

The same principle applies in the spiritual world. All of us are in a situation where we will eventually die without help, and there's nothing we can do to save ourselves. You could thrash around in the freezing water, you could try to operate on yourself, but all of your efforts would be futile.

All of our efforts won't help us spiritually, either, but God is willing to save us—if we will only believe in Him.

God saved you by his special favor when you believed.
And you can't take credit for this;
it is a gift from God.
EPHESIANS 2:8

CONFIDENCE

Your self-esteem should not be derived from how great you think you are but from how much God loves you.

There is a lot of talk these days about building your "self-esteem" so you will have confidence to make it in society. But confidence placed in yourself is doomed for failure (because you'll someday learn that you aren't as great as you have been telling yourself). Instead of being confident in yourself, try placing your confidence in God, Who will never fail you.

If you belong to God, there is no one or nothing that can separate you from His love and protection. This can give you real confidence. Circumstances can be tough, but He will see you through. Even death won't defeat you.

God loves you so much that He allowed His Son to die on the cross for you. That is the kind of love in which you can place all of your confidence.

I am convinced that nothing can ever separate us from his love. Death can't, and life can't. The angels can't, and the demons can't. Our fears for today, our worries about tomorrow, and even the powers of hell can't keep God's love away.
ROMANS 8:38

PLEASING GOD

Discover the things that please God, and then make them habits.

It's only natural to want to please someone you like. You do it, not because you're obligated, but because you want to give joy to someone you care about. God likes it when you please Him, but don't do it to give Him joy—God doesn't need to have His spirits lifted. And don't try to please God in order to butter Him up like you might do to a parent or a boss in order to get something.

Pleasing God is for your enjoyment and your benefit. When you do the things and think the thoughts that please God (to find out how, check God's Word), your life takes on new meaning and purpose. Not only that, but your impact on those around you will increase as you make pleasing God a habit.

---

*And we will receive whatever we request
because we obey him and do the things that please him.*
1 JOHN 3:22

BE CONTENT

It is impossible to weigh your contentment on a scale of stuff. If stuff is your measurement, you will never have enough, because there will always be someone who has more stuff than you do. You will never be content.

Neither will you be content if you are proud of the fact that you don't have a lot of stuff, because there will always be someone who is more proud of their poverty than you are.

Stuff has nothing to do with contentment, because contentment is a matter of your heart, not your wallet. Real contentment comes when you focus your heart and your mind on things above rather than things on Earth (Col. 3:2).

I know how to live on almost nothing or with everything.
I have learned the secret of living in every situation.

LOOKING AT GOD INSTEAD OF YOUR CIRCUMSTANCES

*If you look at your circumstances through God's eyes,
then your circumstances won't obscure your view of God.*

We make life a lot harder than it needs to be. This happens whenever the circumstances in our lives discourage us. When problems arise, and nothing goes right, the stress builds. We become unhappy, discouraged, and discontented. It is in those tough times that God seems distant.

But it doesn't have to be that way. Instead of trying to see God through your circumstances, take the opposite approach. Look at your circumstances through God's eyes.

God doesn't see your circumstances as insurmountable. He's not intimidated or discouraged by them. Since they aren't problems for Him, they shouldn't be for you.

The next time you find yourself looking down in despair, lift your head and start looking up. Stop worrying about your obstacles, and start thinking about the God Who can help you overcome them.

------

*For I can do everything with the help of Christ
who gives me the strength I need.*
PHILIPPIANS 4:13

THE INSIGNIFICANCE OF INSIGNIFICANCE

Whenever you feel insignificant,
remember how important you are to God.

It doesn't take much effort to feel insignificant. Another person—probably someone you know pretty well—makes a negative comment about you, or you fail to meet your own expectations, and soon you're feeling low.

Or you start comparing your mundane achievements to the people who make headlines for their great accomplishments—especially in your field—and it doesn't take long for you to believe that your work or your position doesn't count for much. You wonder if anybody really cares.

Okay, we've gone low enough! That's no place for someone whom God loves and cares about more than can be imagined. Your life has value and what you do has significance because you are important to God.

"Not even a sparrow, worth only half a penny,
can fall to the ground without your Father knowing it.
And the very hairs on your head are all numbered.
So don't be afraid; you are more valuable to him
than a whole flock of sparrows."
MATTHEW 10:29-31

It's Okay to Feel Small

When you begin to feel self-important,
remember how mighty and vast God is.

The opposite of feeling insignificant is feeling self-important, and we've got plenty of that going around. Everybody wants to be king of the world. There's only one problem with putting yourself at the center of the universe: You tend to push God out.

We're all for feeling confident. There's nothing wrong with knowing who you are, as long as you know *Whose* you are. You aren't some autonomous being in full control of your destiny. You belong to God, Who designed and built you as surely as He set the moon and the stars in place.

Knowing that, it seems a little silly to tell God, "Thanks for getting the ball rolling, but I can handle it from here." Instead, we should be thankful that our big God has taken our small lives and turned them into something significant.

When I look at the night sky and see the work of your fingers—
the moon and the stars you have set in place—
what are mortals that you should think of us,
mere humans that you should care for us?
PSALM 8:3–4

AMBITION

If you want to have a great life for yourself,
then give it away to God.

Ambition is natural. After all, you want a happy family, friendships, financial security, and good health. In other words, you want a great life. It's only natural to have such ambitions and to do everything necessary to attain your goals. But should you be ambitious just because it comes naturally?

Jesus taught about the great irony of self-ambition. He said you must lose your life in order to keep it. This paradox forces you to choose which is more important: your physical life or your eternal soul. Jesus taught that gaining everything on Earth—all the things that are supposed to make you happy—will still leave you emotionally bankrupt if you don't have a spiritual relationship with God.

God wants you to live with ambition and purpose, but He doesn't want your focus to be self-centered and self-directed. Let God be your priority. Let living in His Kingdom be your ambition.

"And how do you benefit if you gain the whole world
but lose or forfeit your own soul in the process?"
LUKE 9:25

DO YOU WANT TO
KNOW GOD'S WILL?

If you want to know God's will,
spend time with Him.

One of the mysteries of life is the will of God. We desperately want to know what God wants us to do, but we're not really sure how to find out. While it's true that we'll never know all of God's will (after all, He's God), we can know a lot of what He wants us to do by spending time with Him.

Think about it on a human level. The more you get to know someone, the more you know what that person is like, and the more you know what that person likes. That's what God's will is all about—knowing what God is like and knowing what He likes. So you could say that the only way to really know God's will is to really know God. How do you do that? By reading the Bible, His personal message to you, and by talking with Him as often as you can.

Your word is a lamp for my feet and a light for my path.
PSALM 119:105

ARE YOU GOD'S "FAIR-WEATHER" FRIEND?

*God's unconditional love for us
should be our motivation to love Him.*

Nobody likes a fair-weather friend. You know, those people who hang around only when things are going well. You realize that their companionship and loyalty are merely an illusion if they bolt as soon as times get tough. You wouldn't want a "friend" like that.

Neither does God, but sadly, many of us treat Him that way. We give God our adoration and allegiance only when He fulfills our expectations. So, if things are going smoothly in our lives, we are glad to express our appreciation by being attentive to Him. But when difficulties arise, we are quick to blame God. We want a God Who is going to make our lives easy, so if He won't give us what we want, then we don't want to waste our time on Him.

Aren't you glad that His love for us endures no matter how we treat Him? That is true love from a true friend, and that should be how we respond to Him.

*We know how much God loves us,
and we have put our trust in him.*
1 JOHN 4:16

Seek This First

Next time you write out your priorities,
make sure you put God at the top.

Whenever you set goals for yourself, it's important to prioritize them. Decide which ones are most important, and do these first. Too often we waste our time on lower shelf, easy-to-attain goals when we should be striving for the goals on the top shelf, even if they are harder to reach.

As you get to know God better, you will find that He will ask you to operate at a higher level of living. He wants you to reach for the top shelf. This has nothing to do with moving to the mountains or getting a promotion at work. What it means is that you shouldn't worry about your short-term, personal needs (they're important, but don't let them consume you). Trust God to provide for the everyday stuff, and then make God and His Kingdom—which He is building in this world through the hearts of those who follow Him—your highest priority.

He will give you all you need from day to day
if you live for him and make the Kingdom of God
your primary concern.
MATTHEW 6:33

TWO KINDS OF ANGER

There are two kinds of anger. There is "righteous" anger that comes out of a righteous response to sin. This is the kind of anger that Jesus displayed when He chased the money changers out of the Temple (Mark 11:15–17). You might express this type of anger, too. You can express this emotion and still have God in control of your life. In fact, it is the Holy Spirit inside of you that reacts and controls your responses.

The second kind of anger controls you. You lose your temper. You say or do something you later regret. Don't try to give God credit for this type of anger. He doesn't have anything to do with it (and He doesn't want you to, either). This is the kind of anger that the Bible warns against because it can take over control of your life.

Only God should have control of your life. Make sure that your temper is not pushing Him out of His rightful place.

Don't be quick-tempered,
for anger is the friend of fools.
ECCLESIASTES 7:9

KEEP A BALANCED PERSPECTIVE

*The more you look up to God,
the less you will look down on people.*

Have you ever noticed how poorly people treat each other? We've all been there. We've all said something disparaging about another driver who cut us off in traffic. We've all read an article about some unfortunate soul and said, "He got what he deserved."

Why are we so quick to look down on other people? Is it because there's no other way to make ourselves feel better? That can't be it, because when it comes to others, the only way to improve our lives is to help them.

No, we think it has more to do with God. The less time we spend learning to know God and what He wants us to do, the more time we have to criticize others. On the other hand, the more we invite God into the details of our lives, the more likely we will be to encourage and lift up other people rather than tear them down.

---

*Live a life filled with love for others,
following the example of Christ.*
EPHESIANS 5:2

SIT STILL AND LISTEN

God is more likely to speak to you with a gentle whisper than with a loud voice.

Prayer isn't talking *to* God. Prayer is really talking *with* God. It is a conversation between you and Him; it is a dialogue where you each take turns *talking* as well as *listening*.

Most of our prayers include a lot of our own talking, but they usually lack the important aspect of listening. Of course, we don't mean to suggest that you are going to hear a celestial voice booming in the heavens like the sound of thunder. We don't even think that you'll hear an amplified voice like God speaking through a megaphone. That is not how He works. God usually speaks in quietness. You hear Him, not audibly with your ears, but internally in your heart and soul.

The Holy Spirit is God's voice inside of you. He wants to speak to you, but you need to be quiet for a few moments so you can hear Him.

"Be silent, and know that I am God!"
PSALM 46:10

THE KNIFE OF GOD

The sharpest object you will ever handle is the Word of God.

There's a reason why the Bible is the world's best-selling book and why its message changes millions of lives every year. The Bible is God's Word. The Bible is not a collection of ideas about God that a bunch of people had centuries ago. The Bible is God speaking to you right now. That's why it's so powerful and so full of insight. God knows your inner thoughts and has a message of love and hope just for you. God has great plans for you, and just about all of them are contained in His Word (Jeremiah 29:11).

When you pick up your Bible to read it each day (you are doing that, aren't you?), handle it with care. It isn't just a book, it's a device so sharp and penetrating that it will cut you to the center of your being. The Bible will open you up so God can pour His words into you.

For the word of God is full of living power.
It is sharper than the sharpest knife,
cutting deep into our innermost thoughts and desires.
It exposes us for what we really are.
HEBREWS 4:12

FAITH

Faith placed in God prevails. Faith placed anyway is the fails.

At its core, faith is believing that someone or something will be worthwhile in your life. The problem with the world is not that people lack faith. The problem is that their faith is misplaced. Most people put their faith in things or in people that will someday prove unreliable and unfulfilling. Have you been hesitant to have faith in your future because the people and circumstances in your life are unreliable?

For faith to ultimately work and last, it must be placed in something that will not fail in the future. God is the only unfailing place for your faith. He always makes good on His promises. No one who has ever known Him has found Him to be unfaithful. He will do what He has said. You can hold on to His promises. Nothing and nobody else but God is worthy of your complete trust.

"Have faith in God. . . .
All that's required is that you really believe
and do not doubt in your heart."

MARK 11:22-23

Take God's Commands Personally

Appreciate the commands of Scripture as much as the promises.

How we love the *promises* of God! When you read the Bible and uncover a verse like Hebrews 11:6—"God. . . rewards those who sincerely seek him"—it's like you've found a treasure. Our natural inclination is to want to "claim" a promise of God like a prospector stakes a claim on a rich vein of gold.

But what about the *commands* of Scripture? For some reason we tend to interpret a command like Mark 16:15—"Go into all the world and preach the Good News to everyone, everywhere"—as being more general in nature. Instead of personalizing it, we figure it applies to other people, especially those in full-time Christian service.

Is it okay to take God's promises personally while applying His commands generally? We think you know the answer to that. All of God's Word is personal. All of it—the promises as well as the commands—applies to all of us.

You made me; you created me.
Now give me the sense to follow your commands.
Psalm 119:73

How Can You Help the Most?

The real test of how much you care for your friend is
whether you are willing to confront your friend.

Today we're going to talk about a subject that you aren't going to like: confrontation. It is our humble (but probably correct) opinion that you avoid confrontations. How do we know this? Well, if you are like most people, you don't even have enough nerve to tell someone that they have a piece of spinach stuck between their teeth.

The Bible tells us that we are to confront a friend if we notice some aspect of our friend's life that is contrary to the character of Christ. *Spotting* the fault is not usually the problem. *Saying* something about it is where we get hung up.

Maybe you're reluctant to mention a problem in a friend's life because then your friend may feel the freedom to do the same to you. But you should welcome that kind of confrontation in your life because it will help you stay close to God.

Dear brothers and sisters, if another Christian
is overcome by some sin,
you who are godly should gently
and humbly help that person back onto the right path.
GALATIANS 6:1

Be a Quick Listener

Your willingness to listen is your gift to others.

The most important part of communication is listening. We all know that, yet we are so quick to tell others what we think, and only then do we listen (mainly to hear what they think of what we just said).

Like it does so often, the Bible offers a different way. Listen first, then talk. There are at least two benefits to this pattern. To start with, the only way to learn something is to listen (you will never learn something from your own mouth, unless you want to learn how careless you are with your words). The main advantage of hearing others speak first is that you may realize what you were about to say is completely wrong or meaningless.

The other benefit is that you are less likely to get upset if you listen before you speak. Our own words will incite us much quicker than the words of others.

Be quick to listen, slow to speak,
and slow to get angry.
JAMES 1:19

CONFORMITY

There is tremendous pressure to conform to our culture. Few of us want to stick out where we are subject to ridicule. It is much safer, we think, to blend in and go along with the group mentality. But have you noticed that the group mentality is usually wrong? This shouldn't come as any shock to us, because our own natural instincts are usually just the opposite of how God wants us to respond to any situation.

Check your life to see if society is influencing your thinking. You probably haven't been brainwashed totally, but there is a strong chance that your thinking has been influenced. If you are going to be a fully devoted follower of God, you've got to make sure that you don't conform to the culture in any significant way that would compromise godly principles. A transformation of your thinking process may be required, but God can handle that if you allow Him to.

Don't copy the behavior and customs of this world. . .
Romans 12:2

RENEW YOUR MIND

What you think determines what you do.

The mind is a terrible thing to waste." No kidding. But mere knowledge isn't going to remedy the situation. A lot of brilliant people have done some pretty stupid stuff. Our minds don't need more information to get right. Our minds need transformation.

The only One Who can enter our hearts and transform our minds is God. Fancy philosophers can't do it. Self-help gurus can't do it. Our hard work can't do it. God must change our minds in every detail (don't expect it to happen overnight —it takes time). You aren't a passive part of the mind renewal process. First, you must invite Him to do His work. Then, once you have "learned the truth that is in Jesus. . .there must be a spiritual renewal of your thoughts and attitudes" (Eph. 4:21, 23).

But let God transform you into a new person
by changing the way you think.
ROMANS 12:2

DO WHAT IS GOOD

Motivation can fade. Habits prevail.

Every once in a while, we need to hear a great motivational sermon. It can really recharge our spiritual batteries. But you must avoid becoming a motivational junkie—the kind of person who has to be hyped up emotionally before you can get going. If you become dependent on motivational sermons, you'll fail miserably in your spiritual life. (You'll get weary of the emotional roller coaster. And after a while, all of the sermons will sound the same.)

Instead of depending on someone else to fire you up, get busy helping others. Do it regularly. Make it a part of your life. When "doing good" for others is a habit in your life, then you'll find that it happens regardless of your emotions. You'll find that you're doing these things because they are rewarding (not just because some eloquent speaker psyched you into it).

So don't get tired of doing what is good.
Don't get discouraged and give up,
for we will reap a harvest of blessing
at the appropriate time.
GALATIANS 6:9

CONTROL YOUR ANGER

Control your anger or it will control you.

No emotion ignites quicker than anger. Yes, there is such a thing as love at first sight, but it's rare. Happiness takes a while to unfold, and sadness seems to creep up on you. But anger is a different animal. Someone says the wrong thing, or you see something that upsets you and, *pow*—the anger rises up like a volcano, erupting for all to see. And once it's out there, it's hard to put a cork on your anger.

The Bible instructs us to be slow to anger. It doesn't say we shouldn't get angry, because that would be like saying, "Don't breathe." We're human. We get angry. But when we are thoughtful and patient, hearing others out before making our pronouncements, we are less likely to be foolish or destructive in our anger. Here's another reason to manage our anger: God is pleased when you keep your anger under control.

Your anger can never make things right in God's sight.
JAMES 1:20

JOY

Joy gives you strength in difficult circumstances.
Try to live above it as you may, but you cannot stay there.

Think about being in the presence of the most caring, compassionate, and loving person that you know. Now, multiply that feeling a hundred times, and you may get a sense of what it was like for the disciples to know Jesus.

Are you jealous that Peter, John, and the rest of the gang got to know Jesus personally? Well, don't be. Oh, sure, you can't presently experience the joy of seeing Him face-to-face, but that day will come. And in the meantime, you'll have the joy that comes from having a personal relationship with the Almighty God.

You can connect with God and experience His abundant joy. Don't miss the opportunity.

"Truly, you will weep and mourn
over what is going to happen to me,
but the world will rejoice.
You will grieve, but your grief will suddenly turn to
wonderful joy when you see me again."

JOHN 16:20

CHURCH DIFFERENCES

Don't let your differences separate you from others.

Drive around any town and you'll see lots of different churches: Baptist churches, Presbyterian churches, Methodist churches, Independent Bible churches, Catholic churches, Pentecostal churches, Orthodox churches, and Lutheran churches. It can all be rather confusing.

It's fine that we have different churches with different names and different ways of doing things. Differences are good! It shows that the universal church, composed of all believers everywhere, is a diverse bunch. But we should never let our differences separate us. The Bible says that God sees no distinction between men and women, rich and poor, slave and free, Baptist and Catholic. When we follow His Son, Jesus Christ, He sees us all as one.

This is the church of the living God,
which is the pillar and support of the truth.
1 TIMOTHY 3:15

LOVE BEFORE FIRST SIGHT

God loved you long before you loved Him.

Hollywood movie producers know that the romantic notion of "love at first sight" makes for a good love story. In real life, however, it is nothing more than "attraction at first sight." Real love requires *knowing* a person.

God didn't love you at first sight, because He actually loved you long before you were born. In fact, He loved you before He created the world. Since before the beginning of time, God knew all about you. He has known all along the kind of person you would be. Even though He has known forever all of your weaknesses, He has loved from then until now.

Don't ever think that God loves you because you have decided to love Him. Your love definitely pleases Him, but He is not reciprocating your affection. God has been loving you and awaiting your affection throughout history. Now *that's* a love story.

Long ago, even before he made the world,
God loved us and chose us in Christ
to be holy and without fault in his eyes.
EPHESIANS 1:4

GOD'S WHISPER

If you aren't hearing the voice of God, your life may be too noisy.

People often wonder if God ever speaks in a voice we can hear. Absolutely. There are times when God speaks through other people in order to tell us something. And sometimes God will speak directly to us. So how do we listen to the voice of God?

If we want to hear God's voice, the first thing we need to be is quiet. God won't shout above the cacophony of our lives. As the prophet Elijah discovered, God comes quietly when we least expect Him. God told Elijah to meet Him "on the mountain" (1 Kings 19:11). As Elijah waited, there was a mighty windstorm, an earthquake, and a fire, but the Lord wasn't in any of those. He came to Elijah in "a gentle whisper."

God will come to you in a gentle whisper, too—in your thoughts and in your heart. But you'll never hear God's voice unless you turn off the noise.

And after the fire there was the sound of a gentle whisper.
1 KINGS 19:12

GOSSIP

If someone can't mind their own business,
it may be the due to a small mind and no business of their own.

Gossip and laziness are closely related. Lazy people love to talk about others and stick their noses into other people's business. And if you run across someone who talks a lot about others (one of those "Can you keep a secret?" types), it's likely that person isn't very productive with his or her time.

Christians can get (and deserve) a bad reputation by being lazy gossips. Do you want to improve the perception of Christians and bring honor to God in the process? Then work hard, keep to your own business, and never get tired of doing good. This isn't just good advice. It is what God wants you to do.

Yet we hear that some of you are living idle lives,
refusing to work and wasting time
meddling in other people's business.
In the name of the Lord Jesus Christ,
we appeal to such people—
no, we command them:
Settle down and get to work.
2 THESSALONIANS 3:11–12

Make Your Prayers a Priority

If your prayers don't mean anything to you,
they mean even less to God.

A lot of people pray, but few people pray effectively. When you negotiate with God as if you're making some kind of deal ("God, if You do this, then I'll do such and such"), you're not praying effectively. If you pray only when you're in trouble, you're not praying effectively (God's not a magic genie). Praying when you're exhausted and barely able to keep your eyes open (which means you fall asleep as soon as you close your eyes to pray) is not effective.

Effective prayer doesn't just happen; it takes effort, devotion, and discipline. Think of prayer like a muscle—the more you exercise it, the stronger it will get. On the other hand, if you neglect your prayer muscle for long periods of time and then suddenly activate it only in emergencies, don't be surprised if the results are less than you hope for.

Devote yourselves to prayer with an alert mind
and a thankful heart.
Colossians 4:2

DO YOU LOVE GOD?

You can't honestly say that you love God unless
you know Him and know yourself.

Do you love God? Are you personally involved with Him, or are you just relying on family or social traditions? Is your whole being involved, or are you closing off part of your life from Him?

Do you *love* God? Love means more than just knowing or respecting Him. Are you giving Him a place of priority in your life above everything else? Is it love in words only, or are there actions that prove your love?

Do you love *God?* Do you love just the notion of a celestial being, or do you love the real God Who deserves our devotion? Are you only interested in the parts of Him that you want (like His loving and forgiving nature)? Or, do you love God for all His attributes (such as His righteousness and holiness that abhor sinful behavior)?

Spend this day considering the question: "Do you love God?"

"And you must love the Lord your God with all your heart,
all your soul, all your mind, and all your strength."
MARK 12:30

PREACHERS CAN'T DO IT ALONE

Don't leave the sermon at church.

Have you ever wondered why preachers preach sermons? Are they trying to impress their parishioners, or do they have more noble purposes in mind? Perhaps good sermons delivered eloquently help preachers feel good about all those years they spent in seminary.

We believe the vast majority of preachers prepare and deliver their sermons for one overarching purpose—so those of us sitting in the pews might be motivated to live our lives more for God and less for ourselves. Of course, the preachers can't do it alone, no matter how powerful their sermons. We need to help by taking the sermons with us when we leave the church building.

The church isn't the building anyway. We are the church, and wherever we go, we take the sermons—and all that they mean—with us.

Now wherever we go he uses us to tell others about the Lord
and to spread the Good News like a sweet perfume.
2 CORINTHIANS 2:14

OVERCOME YOUR FEARS

Faith is the antidote for fear.

Fear is an emotion everyone experiences. People fear tangible things like being hurt, robbed, or cheated. They also fear intangible things like rejection, failure, and giving speeches. Even though fear can sometimes be useful, it can easily become your greatest enemy and hold your life in an awesome grip. Fear can keep you from doing the right thing at the right time.

Remember the story when a storm threatened to capsize the boat in which the disciples and Jesus were sailing? Jesus remained calm. He had faith that He could overcome the danger at hand, and He told the disciples that their fear came from a lack of faith.

If you want to overcome your fears, you must have faith that God can conquer them.

When he woke up, he rebuked the wind and said to the water,
"Quiet down!" Suddenly the wind stopped,
and there was a great calm. And he asked them,
"Why are you so afraid? Do you still not have faith in me?"
MARK 4:39–40

SIGNED BY THE ARTIST

Either God made you, or He didn't.

The human body is the most complex organism in the universe. It would take a computer the size of the Empire State Building to duplicate the potential processing power of your brain (notice we said "potential"). The way your bones and muscles, your heart and blood vessels, and your nervous system and organs function is a miracle even to the most skeptical scientists.

You can choose to believe that your amazing body evolved from a slimy swamp creature, but isn't it more logical to believe that an incredibly intelligent and powerful Creator designed your body and your mind? Not only did God make you, but He made you for a purpose. He made you so you could relate to Him while you're living here on Earth, and He made you so you could enjoy Him forever.

Just as an artist signs his work, God has left His imprint in your life. And it's that imprint that gives your life meaning.

So God created people in his own image; God patterned them after himself; male and female he created them.
GENESIS 1:27

NEEDING GOD WHEN YOU THINK YOU DON'T

The time when you need God the most is
the time when you don't think you need Him at all.

You are in real danger the moment you think that you are independent and self-sufficient. If you get to that stage, you are likely to stop relying upon God, and you'll no longer seek His guidance.

This doesn't happen when times are tough (because in difficult situations we realize our need for God's intervention). But when we are at a place and time in life when the circumstances are serene and easy, we can be lulled into a misconception that God isn't necessary. When that happens, then we start making decisions and choices based on our own faulty wisdom instead of God's divine direction.

If things are going well for you, then give praise to God for your present situation. Realize that God (not you) is the One Who is responsible for creating those tranquil circumstances in your life.

Pride goes before destruction, and haughtiness before a fall.
PROVERBS 16:18

THE PASSING OF TIME

Much more than a measure, time is a gift from God.

Unlike the other creatures on Earth, we humans are aware of time. We have memory of the past, we experience the present, and we can plan for the future. Time is God's gift to us. It's a way to measure and celebrate the events of our lives as they unfold. In that sense, time gives us joy. Time also provides a way for us to anticipate things to come. In that sense, time gives us hope.

Time can also give us anxiety, and this is when we need to realize that God wants to be involved in the details of our lives. There is never a time when we can't turn to God and ask for His involvement in our circumstances. When we experience "good times," we need to thank Him. When the days are dark and uncertain, we need to find His blessings. The more we realize that God uses all of our experiences—both good and bad—for our good, the more we will understand how much He loves us (Rom. 8:28).

God has made everything beautiful for its own time.
ECCLESIASTES 3:11

ETERNITY IS IN YOUR HEART

You were made for forever as surely as you were made for time.

Have you ever wondered why you think about forever? You don't just think about tomorrow, or next week, or even next year. In your quiet moments of reflection you think about a time beyond this time and beyond your life, and you wonder what it will be like.

The reason the ideas of "forever" and "ever after" permeate your thinking is that God put them there. He stuck those thoughts in your head and your heart because He wanted you to know that He exists, even though you can't see Him. God also wants you to know that He dwells in a place far beyond the universe He created. It's a place called heaven.

When you dream about heaven and an eternal time beyond this life, you are doing something very natural. What is unnatural is to believe that this life is all there is.

God. . .has planted eternity in the human heart.
ECCLESIASTES 3:11

OUR VIEW IS LIMITED

Rather than worry about what you don't know about God,
concentrate on what you do know.

Humans are a curious bunch, and we're also impatient, a combination that explains why we jump to conclusions so often. This is especially true of our relationship with God. There's so much about Him that we don't know, and rather than being patient and waiting for Him to give us the right information at the appropriate time, we conclude that either He doesn't care about us or isn't able to help us. Both of these conclusions are dead wrong, but it's all we've got because we don't know any more.

The only way to avoid these frustrating conclusions is to concentrate on what we do know about God and trust Him for the rest. We need to trust that He has the world in His hands, and He has us in His hands. We can't see the big picture, but He can, and He's working everything out for our ultimate good.

People cannot see the whole scope of God's work
from beginning to end.
ECCLESIASTES 3:11

SORROW

When God gives us forgiveness, Satan gives us guilt.

There is a fine line between sorrow and guilt. Both emotions can spring from doing something wrong. But the consequences of these two emotions can be drastically different.

God wants you to be sorry when you have done something wrong. Sincere sorrow is part of the process of repentance. It means you regret what you have done and don't want to do it again. With this type of attitude, God can turn your life around and get you back on the right track.

Satan, on the other hand, wants you to go far beyond sorrow. He wants you to feel guilty, and he uses guilt as an oppressive emotion. It will make your conscience heavy and your focus introspective. Guilt ignores the very reason why Jesus died for you: forgiveness.

The next time you regret your actions, thank God. Your sorrow is a sign that Jesus is alive and active in your life.

For God can use sorrow in our lives to help us turn away from
sin and seek salvation.
We will never regret that kind of sorrow.
2 CORINTHIANS 7:10

THE REALITY OF ETERNITY

God didn't create eternity for you; He created you for eternity.

Did you know that you were made for eternity? That's why you can't help thinking about it. God literally created you so you could live forever. There's only one problem. Sin got in the way. In effect, sin voided God's eternal warranty on your life (Rom. 6:23). Unless you deal with the sin problem (and it's a big problem), you'll never live to see forever (at least not forever with God).

Ah, but there's a way to deal with the sin problem. When you accept "the free gift of God. . .eternal life through Christ Jesus our Lord" (Rom. 6:23), God automatically restores your eternal warranty and puts you back on track for forever. All of this is because of Jesus, "the living one who died," so that death could be defeated on your behalf—forever!

"Don't be afraid! I am the First and the Last.
I am the living one who died.
Look, I am alive forever and ever!
And I hold the keys of death and the grave.
REVELATION 1:17–18

WHO IS GOD?

The character of God is not determined by your perceptions of Him.

Some people form their beliefs about God based on their personal opinions. This is nothing more than *gastrointestinal theology* (having a "gut feeling" about God). Unfortunately, gut feelings are usually the result of indigestion rather than divine inspiration.

God isn't going to change His character to conform to what we think about Him. He is not like a celestial Mr. Potato Head that we get to design; we don't get to rearrange His features to suit our momentary whims and transitory opinions.

God is Who He is. Our opinions of Him should not be determined by what we want Him to be (or by what foods we eat). Instead, our understanding and beliefs about God should be based upon what we learn about Him from the Bible. Make sure your concept of Who God is conforms to what God says about Himself.

This is what the LORD says: . . . "Let them boast in this alone:
that they truly know me and understand that
I am the LORD who is just and righteous,
whose love is unfailing, and that I delight in these things."

CHARACTER COUNTS

Others determine your reputation. You determine your character.

One of the great debates of the last few years has centered on character. Some people believe that it's possible for a person to possess both a public and a private character, even if the two are very different. What you do in private, the reasoning goes, is your business, as long as it doesn't affect your public performance.

There's only one problem with this thinking. Once you divide your personality and your actions into two or more categories or compartments, you deviate from the very definition of character. At its root, character is defined by integrity, and at the heart of integrity is the idea of wholeness.

One of the best ways to keep your life whole is to pay attention to the small stuff. Do what it takes every day to develop your character and preserve your integrity. Most of all, don't live your life to please others. Live your life to please God.

May integrity and honesty protect me,
for I put my hope in you.
PSALM 25:21

SECURITY

*No amount of money can match the value of God's love
or the price that was paid for your salvation.*

Many people look to their own financial resources for their security. They believe they have to take care of themselves, so they devote all of their efforts to earning and saving money. At some point, however, reliance solely on finances can be misplaced and out of proportion. How should you maintain the proper balance?

Here's a simple test to determine whether or not you are depending on God or on money for your security: "Wherever your treasure is, there your heart and thoughts will also be" (Luke 12:34). If your treasure is money, you will be plagued with anxieties about losing it every time the NASDAQ takes a tumble. On the other hand, if your real treasure is your relationship with God, the focus of your life will be on Him.

Put your treasure in the Kingdom of God which will last forever (and pays great dividends).

*"Yes, a person is a fool to store up earthly wealth
but not have a rich relationship with God."*

LUKE 12:21

LIFE IS A MARATHON

*It's better to see the circumstances of your life
in the long run than the short-term.*

When stuff you don't like happens outside your control, you shouldn't blame God, or worse, assume that He can't do anything about it. God is always aware of what is happening to you, and He is never powerless to help you.

So why do bad things happen to you? Honestly—and this isn't a weak approach—there are times when you just don't know. Other times, especially when the bad things are the consequences of your own sins, you know exactly why stuff is happening. Either way you need to believe that the end results will be for your own good if (and this is a big "if") you love God and submit to Him in all areas of your life.

Remember that life is a marathon, not a sprint. The pain you are feeling today is just part of the overall race, and the prize is guaranteed if you cross the finish line.

---

*God blesses the people who patiently endure testing.
Afterward they will receive the crown of life that
God has promised to those who love him.*
JAMES 1:12

BUSY-NESS

Never mistake activity for achievement.

There is a principle of economics that goes something like this: If you lose money on every sale, you can't make up for it in quantity. In other words, if your product is bad, it is not going to get better just because you make more of it.

Some people need to apply this principle to the activities of their lives. They mistakenly think that increasing their commitments is admirable because "more is better." But sometimes more is worse, and this is particularly true of activities in our daily schedule.

Before you get busier than you already are, evaluate what you are doing. Maybe you should delete some commitments from your schedule so that you can do a better job with fewer activities.

Whatever you do, do well.
ECCLESIASTES 9:10

DESTRUCTIVE CRITICISM

*It's impossible to offer destructive criticism
and love someone at the same time.*

Whereas constructive criticism can be encouraging and helpful to others, most criticism is quite destructive. Destructive criticism attempts to deflect the attention from the real issue, which might be something as basic as jealousy. Destructive criticism takes the attention away from the person doing the criticizing, and that may be where the real problem lies. Destructive criticism also comes out of a heart where love is lacking, at least in that moment.

Love is actually the antidote for destructive criticism for this reason. Destructive criticism is motivated by fear—fear of being discovered, fear of being criticized, or fear of having to be open and honest. When you are motivated by love, you are less likely to be critical of others, because you'll have their best interests in mind.

Such love has no fear because perfect love expels all fear.
1 JOHN 4:18

CREATION

Darwinists keep looking for the missing link.
The link they are missing is Christ's role in creation.

The issue of "origins" is a favorite topic of debate for scientists, philosophers, and theologians. If the subject of creation interests you, be careful that you aren't so engrossed in the theories that you ignore the obvious conclusions.

There may be legitimate questions about the "when" and the "how" of creation, but there is no doubt about "who" created all things. The Bible says that God created our universe (Gen. 1:1). But more specifically, the Bible clarifies that Christ had a primary role in the creation of the world. He was the intelligent designer and the master builder in the whole process.

When you contemplate the enormity of the universe or the intricacies of nature, remember Who was responsible for it.

Christ is the one through whom God
created everything in heaven and earth. . . .
Everything has been created through him and for him.
He existed before everything else began,
and he holds all creation together.
COLOSSIANS 1:16–17

LISTEN AND LEARN

Teachers and mentors won't find you; you have to find them.

God sends others to help you grow as a Christian. First and foremost, He sends the Holy Spirit, Who "leads into all truth" (John 14:17). The Holy Spirit is part of the supernatural package of your salvation, so you don't have to go looking for Him.

God also sends people to teach you His truth and to come alongside of you as your spiritual friends and mentors. These people are your pastor, your Bible study leader, the person who is discipling you, and others you will meet along your spiritual journey. God has equipped them to feed you solid spiritual food so you can grow as a Christian.

Even though God does the sending, you have to do the looking. It's up to you to find a local Bible-teaching church. You are responsible to seek out spiritual leaders. Then you need to listen and learn.

But you must remain faithful to the things you have been taught.
You know they are true,
for you know you can trust those who taught you.
2 TIMOTHY 3:14

LISTENING FOR GOD'S VOICE

*God is more likely to speak to you in a gentle whisper
than in a loud voice.*

It is easy to see and hear God in the big events of life—like the birth of a child, avoiding injury in an automobile accident, or deciding to change jobs. But monumental or cataclysmic events don't happen very often. If we expect to hear God only in the spectacular moments, we will miss most of what He is trying to say to us.

Most of the time our lives are filled with common circumstances. Because God wants to be in constant communication with us, He talks to us during those times as well. Listen for Him as you drive to the next appointment, walk to the mailbox, and sit in your living room.

If you listen for God only in the big events, you won't hear Him very often. Try listening for Him in the ordinary routine of your life as well, and you'll be surprised at how much He wants to tell you.

*"Anyone who is willing to hear should listen and understand!
And be sure to pay attention to what you hear.
The more you do this, the more you will understand."*
MARK 4:23–24

FAMILY NAMES

A person's name can tell you a lot about him.

We live in a time when family names are not held in high regard. We're not saying that people are ashamed of their names. They just don't know much about them. The main reason we don't take more pride in our family names is that we don't know our family heritage, and we don't know the meaning of our names. It doesn't take much to dig up some information on your family name, and you may be surprised at what you find. You may also connect with some relatives you never knew you had!

When it comes to both the heritage and the meaning of your name, you can either ignore it or live up to it. And if there isn't much to live up to, then determine to bring honor to your family name.

A good name is more desirable than great riches.
PROVERBS 22:1 NIV

HYPOCRISY

*Be more concerned with how you look to God
than how you look in the mirror.*

A hypocrite is a person who pretends to be different from what he or she really is. When Jesus was on Earth, there were no bigger phonies than the religious leaders (scribes and Pharisees). They portrayed themselves as being holy and righteous because they followed technical rituals (that they made up themselves). Jesus called them hypocrites because they bragged about their extreme habits of cleanliness, but internally, where it mattered, their motives were evil and filthy. The scribes and Pharisees were concerned only with what other people saw on the outside. They failed to realize that God is interested in what is happening on the inside.

Centuries later, many of us are acting like the scribes and Pharisees. We put on a good show on the outside, but our thoughts and attitudes are not pleasing to God. We may be able to fool other people, but we can't fool God.

*"You try to look like upright people outwardly,
but inside your hearts are filled with
hypocrisy and lawlessness."*

MATTHEW 23:28

WHO IS JESUS?

Jesus is the greatest person you will ever meet.

Who is Jesus? He is God's Son, completely perfect yet able to identify with our weaknesses. Jesus is the most extraordinary person ever to live on Earth, and God has raised Him up to the heights of heaven, where He is worthy of the highest praise that heaven and Earth can deliver. Jesus came to Earth to be like us so He could defeat sin, Satan, and death on our behalf. Jesus is greater than all other beings, yet He suffered for us so He could help us with our deepest needs.

Sometimes we use Jesus and God interchangeably, and sometimes we refer to them as two distinct beings. Both are true. Jesus is equal to God in every respect. In fact, Jesus said, "Anyone who has seen me has seen the Father!" (John 14:9).

The Son reflects God's own glory,
and everything about him represents God exactly.
He sustains the universe by the mighty power of his command.
HEBREWS 1:3

GRAB THE TOWEL

*Be more concerned about the task to be performed by you
than the title to be conferred upon you.*

Remember the story of Jesus washing the feet of the disciples? (See John 13:1–11.) It was the custom to wash the feet of guests who had been traveling on the dusty roads. The disciples weren't doing the job, so Jesus got busy and did the task Himself. What makes this incident so ironic is that the disciples had been arguing earlier about which of them was going to be "greatest" in God's Kingdom. While they were worried about a title, Jesus grabbed the towel.

We can't be too critical of the disciples, because we make the same mistake. We're so anxious to be important, to be noticed, and to have prestige. We're thinking so much about our own image that we overlook the needs of others.

Let Jesus be your example. Forget about your own self-importance and focus on the needs of others. Be looking for ways that you can be helpful.

"The greatest among you must be a servant."
MATTHEW 23:11

STAY AT IT EVERY DAY

Discipline begins with small things done daily.

Mark Twain once said: "The secret of getting ahead is getting started. The secret of getting started is breaking your complex tasks into small manageable tasks, and then starting on the first one." That's good advice, whether you want to finish a short-term project, or you desire to get good at something over a long period of time.

Knowing God doesn't happen overnight; it takes a lifetime. And it starts with one small task (such as reading the Bible for fifteen minutes each day) repeated over and over again. Remember that the heart of discipline is repetition, not completion. Don't get discouraged if you don't "get ahead" as soon as you would like. On the other hand, don't just discipline yourself for the sake of discipline. Have a goal in mind—such as knowing God better—so that your daily routine of discipline takes on meaning.

Without wavering,
let us hold tightly to the hope we say we have,
for God can be trusted to keep his promise.
HEBREWS 10:23

FREEDOM FROM SIN

God did His part in freeing you from sin;
you have to do your part in giving it up.

When you accept Jesus as your Savior, you are set free from the penalty of sin. You are also freed from the control of sin. But that does not mean that you are free from the choice of sin.

As long as you live in a world where sin and Satan are present, you will daily face opportunities to choose thoughts, language, and conduct that displease God. Before you belonged to God, you were entrapped by your sin nature. But with your salvation, you were not only freed from sin's eternal death penalty, but you were also freed from the snare of sin. You are really free to choose godly living in every situation.

What kind of choices will you be making today?

Thank God! Once you were slaves of sin. . . .
But now you are free from the power of sin
and have become slaves of God.
Now you do those things that lead to holiness
and result in eternal life.

STRETCH YOURSELF

Once in a while, set a goal that absolutely terrifies you.

If you reach every goal you set, you aren't setting the right kind of goals. Some people think that writing out a "to do" list every few days qualifies as goal setting. Sorry, that just doesn't cut it. A "to do" list is more like a series of duties—things you need to get done just to keep up with life.

By contrast, a goal is something that adds to your life by stretching you to accomplish something you didn't think you could do. Reaching goals takes time, and some goals require a lifetime to reach. If you've never set a goal that brings fear into your heart, you are missing out on one of the great joys of life.

A terrifying goal doesn't have to be dangerous (in fact, for liability purposes, we want to go on record as saying it *shouldn't* be dangerous). But it should stretch you so far that you wonder how you will ever reach it.

So we make it our goal to please him.
2 CORINTHIANS 5:9 NIV

No Religion Necessary

God doesn't give us rules for how to live;
He gives us reasons for how to live.

You probably know a lot of people who want nothing to do with religion. Don't be too quick to criticize them for their attitudes; they might have the right idea.

God doesn't want your life occupied with a lot of religious hoopla that you perform out of tradition without any sense of personal significance. If your "religion" is just a bunch of "do's and don'ts," then God isn't interested in it. (And maybe that's why your spiritual life has seemed so dry and unfulfilling.)

God wants your genuine faith, not your meaningless rituals. He wants you to respond to Him out of love, not out of compulsion, or guilt, or habit. He wants you to enjoy the freedom of faith, without dreading rigid rules.

Stop doing "religious" activities simply because you feel you have to. Instead, take pleasure in your liberty to worship God as a natural expression of your love for Him.

"And you will know the truth,
and the truth will set you free."
JOHN 8:32

THE ROLE OF GOVERNMENT

God doesn't ask you to agree with those who govern you,
but He does ask you to obey them and pray for them.

It's very easy to blur the lines between our faith and our politics, but nowhere in Scripture does God tell us to elect and support only those people who agree with our theological positions. God tells us to submit to them (Titus 3:1), obey them (Rom. 13:1), and pray for them (1 Tim. 2:2).

Even Jesus, who lived on Earth at a time when the Roman government openly oppressed and persecuted Christians, He never called for His followers to overthrow or even disobey the government, even though many in the crowds were hoping He would do that. Instead, Jesus told people they needed a change of heart, not a change in government.

Just as we trust God to rule in our hearts, we need to trust Him by obeying those who rule over us, even if we disagree.

Remind your people to submit to
the government and its officers.
They should be obedient,
always ready to do what is good.
TITUS 3:1

DOUBT

*But when you ask him, be sure that you really expect him to answer,
for a doubtful mind is as unsettled as a wave of the sea.*

You probably wouldn't think that wisdom and doubt were opposites, but they are. The opposite of wisdom is not stupidity because wisdom has nothing to do with intelligence. It's more about being sure that what you are doing is right, which would make the opposite more like uncertainty, or doubt.

To have doubt is to be unsettled, like a wave driven by the wind. To be wise is to trust someone who not only has more experience than you do but who also has your best interests in mind.

When you have doubts in your life, you can go to God for the answers. Be confident that He can handle the problem (or give you the wisdom to). Don't keep fretting about the problem once you have given it to God. From that point on, be confident that He is in charge.

*But when you ask him,
be sure that you really expect him to answer,
for a doubtful mind is as unsettled as a wave of the sea
that is driven and tossed by the wind.*

Your Body and Your Mind

A healthy body and a sharp mind usually go together.

Did you know that there is a direct relationship between your physical fitness and your spiritual life? We're not saying that the fittest people are the most spiritual, or that unfit people are spiritually weak. You may not be able to do anything to improve your physical condition, yet you have every opportunity to grow spiritually.

However, if your body is run down because of the choices you make—such as eating poorly, never getting enough sleep, or rarely exercising—then your mind won't be at its sharpest. And if your mind is dull, then you won't be at your best spiritually (if you don't think so, try reading the Bible when you're dead tired).

God wants you to have a healthy body so you can have a healthy mind, because a healthy mind enables you to love God even more (Matt. 22:37).

God bought you with a high price.
So you must honor God with your body.
1 Corinthians 6:20

LITTLE THINGS

It is only natural that you want to do great things for God. After all that He has done for you, you want to do something significant in return. You want to prove how much you love Him by doing something great and glorious for Him.

Well, stop watching and waiting for some magnificent ministry opportunity. You aren't likely to speak at a Billy Graham Crusade, or drive a Hummer filled with missionaries into the Peruvian rain forest. Just be faithful with the seemingly small things in your life.

Being faithful with the small things *is* a "big" thing. Loving your family, being kind to a stranger, helping a neighbor—these are small things that have great significance in God's eyes.

God doesn't often give us huge opportunities that are spectacular. But He always gives us small opportunities that are significant.

And the King will tell them, 'I assure you,
when you did it to one of the least of
these my brothers and sisters, you were doing it to me!'

BEST FRIENDS

*Your best friends will criticize you privately
and encourage you publicly.*

There is a place for constructive criticism, and we all need it. None of us is above the objective, truthful, and loving correction of someone who has our best interests in mind. This is where your friends come in.

What kind of friends do you have? Do you have friends who will tell you the truth in love (Eph. 4:15), or do you surround yourself with people who tell you what you want to hear? If these are the only friends you have, they're probably not your friends at all, because even though they talk nice in front of you, they're talking about you behind your back.

Your best friends will level with you, even at the risk of alienating you for a while. They'll tell you privately where you're wrong and where you need to straighten up, as long as you let them know ahead of time that you want the truth.

---

*"I am warning you!
If another believer sins, rebuke him;
then if he repents, forgive him."*
LUKE 17:3

KINDNESS

*The time for kindness is when others need it,
not when it is convenient for you.*

In a world of selfishness and violence, kindness is in short supply. That's why any act of kindness, no matter how small, is newsworthy.

Jesus established the standard for kindness when He said, "Love your neighbor as yourself" (Luke 10:27). This principle can give you a quick and easy test to determine whether you are showing kindness to others. In any situation, you can just ask yourself, "How would I like to be treated?" The answer will be obvious to you, and then you can treat others in that same way.

Make every effort this day to show to others the kindness that God wants (and expects) of you.

*"Now which of these three would you say was a neighbor
to the man who was attacked by bandits?" Jesus asked.
The man replied, "The one who showed him mercy."
Then Jesus said, "Yes, now go and do the same."*
LUKE 10:36–37

INTEGRITY IS
SOMETHING YOU ARE

The first step to having integrity is thinking about it.

The mind is a powerful thing. The Bible says that you are what you think about (Prov. 23:7). Read that again. Not only do you *act upon* what you think about, but you also *become* what you think about.

Take the matter of integrity, which is the centerpiece of your character. Integrity is not something you do; it's something you are—a person of integrity. You don't have integrity because you do things that are truthful and honorable and right. You do the right things because you have integrity.

How do you become a person of integrity? You must first think about the things that define integrity. When you occupy your mind with the right things, you will do the right things. You can count on that. You can also be sure that the opposite is true.

Fix your thoughts on what is true and honorable and right.
PHILIPPIANS 4:8

PICTURE THIS

Use your imagination to think about the beauty of God seen His creation.

When you think about truth and honor, you are thinking about concepts. You can't picture truth unless you imagine yourself being truthful. Another part of your thinking involves objects. In your mind you can picture things of purity and beauty, whether you've actually seen or read about them in a book.

When we say the words "quiet mountain stream" or "brilliant beach sunset," wonderful images immediately flash into our minds. You can do the same thing. By using your imagination, you can bring beautiful objects and places into your head.

Be aware of the beauty and detail of God's creation. Read God's Word daily. The more beauty you see or read about with your eyes, the more beauty you will hold in your mind.

Think about things that are pure and lovely and admirable.

Do Your Part;
Let God Do His

You are responsible for the depth of your spiritual understanding.
God is responsible for the breadth of your ministry.

An athlete knows that it takes years of training and practice in order to compete in the Olympics. Everyone knows that you must master the basics of a sport before you can play at a high level of competition.

How come we forget this principle when we think about serving God? We want to accomplish wonderful things for God before we have adequately prepared ourselves. Instead of worrying so much about what we can do for God, we should be concerned with getting to know Him better.

We don't have to postpone sharing our faith with others until we have obtained an advanced degree in theology. But we shouldn't let a desire for a prominent ministry displace the priority of knowing God better. As we gain a deeper understanding of Who He is, then He will open the doors for us to serve Him.

Jesus called out to them, "Come, be my disciples,
and I will show you how to fish for people!"
MATTHEW 4:19

GOD GETS THE CREDIT

You can think about yourself being truthful, and you can imagine objects of beauty. But what is it like to think of something or someone that is worthy of praise?

When you look at an object of beauty—say, a beautiful painting—do you give credit to the painting for its beauty? Oh, you can talk about the painting and rave about its value as an art object, but you can't credit the painting for creating itself.

The credit goes to the artist, who painted this thing of beauty. The artist deserves your admiration because the artist is worthy—you can see the result in front of you. The same thing goes for God, the great Artist Who created the earth and everything in it. He's the One Who is worthy of praise, not the creation.

*So they worshipped the things God made
but not the Creator himself, who is to be praised forever. Amen.*
ROMANS 1:25

Think about Heaven

*Use your imagination to think about what God
has prepared for you.*

Your imagination is a gift from God. Your imagination allows you to think about images that are so real you think you can touch them, even though you have never seen them with your eyes.

There is no image more worthy of your imagination than heaven. We all think about heaven from time to time—we can't help it (Eccles. 3:11)—but too often we limit our imagination to "streets of gold" (Rev. 21:21) and "mansions" (John 14:2 KJV). It's okay to think about heaven the way you would think about Disneyland, with castles, fantasy lands, and thrill rides. But don't limit your thoughts to the happiest place on Earth. Heaven will be much more than we have ever seen or could ever imagine (1 Cor. 2:9).

When you fill your mind with the infinite possibilities of heaven, you have no choice but to think about God.

---

*Let heaven fill your thoughts.
Do not think only about things down here on earth.*
COLOSSIANS 3:2

CAPTIVE THOUGHTS

Thought control has a negative connotation. None of us wants someone else to tell us what to think. During the Cold War, people talked about how the Communists were using propaganda and "thought control" to manipulate the citizenry. Consequently, we'd like to think we can and should control our own thoughts.

If we were to be completely open and honest, we would admit that we aren't very good at controlling our thoughts. If our thoughts were printed out for all to read, we would be pretty embarrassed. It's not as though we're plotting to overthrow governments or wondering how to do nasty things to people. It's those little wanderings into the dark corners of our hearts and minds that are the constant problem. That's why we need to ask God to control our thoughts, which He will do through the Holy Spirit, Who will teach us and remind us of everything God has told us (John 14:26).

And we take captive every thought
to make it obedient to Christ.

INTEGRITY

If you expand the truth, your credibility contracts.

You know you shouldn't lie, but there are many circumstances in life when the truth may seem irrelevant. Is absolute honesty required at all times? Are you obligated to limit your promises to the ones you actually intend to keep? Must you restrict your comments to those that are entirely truthful?

The culture in Jesus' time was so accustomed to making false statements that people would often "swear" to be telling the truth. They assumed that taking an oath of honesty would give greater credibility to their statements. Jesus condemned this custom. He taught that integrity and truth have only one level (Matt. 5:33–37).

Your word should be enough. Jesus wants your words to be truthful in every conversation. Honesty, integrity, and truthfulness should be more than mere concepts for you. God wants you to put them into practice, and He wants them to be defining characteristics of your life.

But most of all, my brothers and sisters, never take an oath,
by heaven or earth or anything else.
Just say a simple yes or no.
JAMES 5:12

KNOWING GOD

*Knowing God takes tremendous effort,
but the reward is great.*

Spiritual growth is not a matter of trying harder. You can't force spirituality. You can't make it happen. It comes as the result of training—developing habits of godliness that are pursued daily.

The spiritual disciplines of prayer and Bible reading are part of the training process. Don't view them as daily chores that must be endured (and that can be checked off your "to do" list as soon as they over). Consider them as an opportunity—a privilege—that allows you to come closer into God's presence and dialogue with Him.

As with any training program, the initial stages are the toughest. But just as you begin to make the activities a regular part of your routine, you'll start to realize the benefits of your diligence.

There is no greater reward than knowing God. He is worth your effort.

*Jesus replied, "Your problem is that you don't know the Scriptures,
and you don't know the power of God."*

Jesus' Authority

*The Word of God heard from your mouth is
more effective if it is also seen in your life.*

When people heard Jesus teach, they were amazed. They had listened many times to the religious leaders who read the Scriptures and gave explanations that were dry, lifeless, and mostly irrelevant.

But Jesus' manner of teaching was different, and so was His content. He explained the Scriptures in a way that made them relevant to life. Jesus spoke with authority because He knew the Scripture. The people could see from the actions of His life that He believed what He taught.

Is your life more like the lives of the religious leaders or like Jesus? When you talk about spiritual matters, do you make them sound dry and lifeless? Or can you communicate the truth about God in a way that makes it seem exciting and appealing to others? Your answers to these questions will depend upon how much you know, and believe, about God. If He is at work in your life, then what you say about Him will be authentic.

*They were amazed at his teaching,
for he taught as one who had real authority—
quite unlike the teachers of religious law.*
MARK 1:22

WHAT WOULD JESUS DO?

*If you're going to compare yourself to anyone,
compare yourself to Jesus.*

The greatest person who ever walked the earth was Jesus. The life of Christ as told in the Bible truly is the Greatest Story Ever Told. Yet Jesus is more than a person, and His life is more than a story.

Jesus is God with skin on, the Creator of the universe in human form. The Bible says that God is a Spirit (John 4:24), which is why no one has seen God. But we have seen Jesus, Who became one of us so that we could see God more clearly (John 1:18).

Jesus experienced all of our temptations and human frailties, yet He lived a perfect life. That's why we can look to Jesus as our example for living. In fact, we must look to Him and His life if we are going to identify with God at all.

*Those who say they live in God should
live their lives as Christ did.*
1 JOHN 2:6

PASSION AND COMPASSION

*You don't have real passion for God unless
you have compassion for people.*

Sometimes we focus so much on God that we forget
about other people. Somehow we get confused and think that
a relationship with God only involves the spiritual realm and
has nothing to do with the "real world." But that is flawed
thinking. God doesn't want us to ignore the "real world." He
wants us to bring a spiritual dimension into it.

You have only to examine the life of Jesus to realize
that God does not want us isolated in some monastery (or
even the church sanctuary) instead of the mall. Jesus walked
the streets and met the people. He was moved with compassion and responded to the hurts and needs of the people. He
didn't cloister Himself in the temple. He connected with people and brought the Kingdom of God to them.

Worship God today by connecting with the people
around you and letting them see God's nature in you.

---

*The unfailing love of the LORD never ends!
By his mercies we have been kept from complete destruction.*
LAMENTATIONS 3:22

DON'T NEGLECT YOUR LIFE

Anything within the scope of your responsibility will decay without your attention.

There's a great principle of the natural world everyone needs to know. It's called the Law of Entropy, and it goes like this: Over time, things naturally lose energy, decay, or move from order to disorder. To illustrate this principle, picture your desk. From time to time you clean your desk, and the reason you clean it repeatedly is because it doesn't stay clean. It moves from order (neat) to disorder (cluttered) for reasons no one really knows.

There are many more examples we could use (garages, closets, cars, hair), but let's focus on some of the intangible things of your life, things like character and integrity. If you leave these areas alone and fail to give them attention, they will lose energy, decay, and move from order to disorder. In fact, anything that requires your time and energy—such as your relationship with God—will go backward if you neglect it.

You must warn each other every day. . .
so that none of you will be deceived by sin.
HEBREWS 3:13

YOUR LOVE

*There is nothing you have that is of any interest to God—
except your love.*

It's impossible to love God as much as He loves us, because by His very nature, God is love. He doesn't have to try to love us. He can do nothing else. On the other hand, our love is fickle. We love when we feel like it, and that includes loving God. Yet we are commanded to love God. In fact, loving God is the most important instruction that Jesus ever gave (Mark 12:30).

Your love for God should not be halfhearted. You should commit yourself to it completely: with your heart (feelings), your soul (spirit), your mind (intellect), and your strength (action).

Loving God is a lifelong process that involves the entire being. Nothing should be held back. Is there some part of you that hasn't yet been given to God? Are you loving Him halfheartedly?

---

*This is real love. It is not that we loved God,
but that he loved us and sent his Son
as a sacrifice to take away our sins.*
1 JOHN 4:10

HAVE FAITH IN GOD

Having faith is essential to living,
but having faith in God is essential to living forever.

Do you know that it's possible to have faith in faith? We may not set out to trust in our belief, but that can easily happen. Here's how it works. We start out in our spiritual lives with a desire to serve God, and somewhere along the line we read, "It is impossible to please God without faith" (Heb. 11:6). So we start having faith in faith.

We start believing that our faith is what saves us and our faith is what keeps us going. Wrong! Faith is what gets us to the One Who saves us and to the One Who keeps us going. What good is it just to have faith? Unless our faith points to the all-powerful, all-loving, totally just, completely holy God of the universe, it won't do us any good. Don't have faith in faith. Have faith in God.

So you see, it isn't enough just to have faith.

GET ON THE PLANE

It's one thing to have faith,
and another matter entirely to act on your faith.

Your faith becomes meaningful to you and effective for your salvation only when you have faith in God. But what if you never act on that faith? How meaningful and effective is it then? Look at it this way. Let's say you made a reservation to fly to Hawaii. When the day for your flight arrives, you drive to the airport, check in, and walk to your gate. But rather than taking your seat on the plane, you sit in the airport and watch the plane take off. Then you turn to some guy next to you and say, "Hey, you see that plane? I have a reservation for that flight. My reservation is going to Hawaii."

Your faith in God is like that reservation to Hawaii. Just as you fulfill your reservation to Hawaii by getting on the plane, you fulfill your faith in God by getting with His plan (Eph. 2:10).

Faith that doesn't show itself by good deeds
is no faith at all—
it is dead and useless.
JAMES 2:17

BE A GOOD DOER

*Something becomes meaningful when it goes from
your head to your heart to your hands.*

Most people think about doing good stuff, and some even have a burden to give their time and resources to something significant. But thinking about something and having a passion for something doesn't mean a thing until you actually go out there and do it.

As Christians, we have a responsibility to turn our thinking into action because it shows the world that our faith in God really matters. Too many of us are content to leave God in heaven. Our faith is tied more to the future than to the present. The truth is, faith is both. It is the "assurance" of what we believe God is going to do in the future, and it is the "evidence" of what God wants to do through us here on Earth (Heb. 11:1).

Others will see our faith in action before they see our faith in heaven.

*"I can't see your faith if you don't have good deeds,
but I will show you my faith through my good deeds."*
JAMES 2:18

IN SEARCH OF SELF-WORTH

Find your self-worth in God's unconditional love for you,
not in your accomplishments.

Our society holds "self-esteem" in great esteem. We want everyone to have a strong self-image. Even the smallest accomplishments are praised at home, at school, and on the job so that everyone has a sense of self-worth. Criticism and competition are condemned if they would jeopardize someone's self-esteem.

But the Bible isn't as politically correct as our society would prefer. It lays the truth on the line: We are all sinners. We are fatally flawed. There is not one good thing about us.

Does the Bible's blatant honesty squash your self-esteem? It shouldn't. The Bible also tells us that we are loved by God. That's where we should find our sense of self-worth. Not in what we have accomplished, but in the fact that God loves us. We are special not on our own but because we are special to Him.

"For God so loved the world that he gave his only Son,
so that everyone who believes in him
will not perish but have eternal life."
JOHN 3:16

PRAYER

The best things to pray about are the things that you care about.

You have a lot going on in your life, including problems, needs, and big decisions. God wants to be included in all of it, but that can happen only through prayer. Prayer is simply talking to God, but sometimes it is hard to get started. What if you can't think of what to say, or how to say it?

Try beginning your prayers by thanking God for Who He is and the world He has created. You should also say that you are sorry for the wrong things that you have done. You can pray for others, asking that God will help them in their difficult circumstances. And last but certainly not least, you shouldn't hesitate one little bit to ask for God's help with your problems—the big ones and the small stuff.

Prayer is your direct link to God. He is waiting, and He is listening. All you have to do is start talking.

"But when you pray, go away by yourself,
shut the door behind you, and pray to your Father secretly.
Then your Father, who knows all secrets, will reward you. . . .
because your Father knows exactly
what you need even before you ask him!"

THE SOUL OF STEWARDSHIP

God doesn't need your money,
but you need to give your money to God.

There is a good barometer for telling how you feel about God: money. This isn't about how much you give. God is more interested in your *attitude* about giving than the *amount* you give. Your attitude about money reveals much about your relationship with God.

"Stewardship" is the way in which you handle what God has given to you. You want to be a good steward of His blessings, but stewardship means much more than being wise with your money and then throwing a few bucks into the offering plate. Stewardship involves realizing that everything you have comes from God. Stewardship requires that you give to God the firstfruits, not the leftovers. And you should consider stewardship a privilege, not a chore.

God won't force you to give back a portion of what He has given you, but He promises to bless you if you do.

"Bring all the tithes into the storehouse
so there will be enough food in my Temple.
If you do," says the LORD Almighty,
"I will open the windows of heaven for you."
MALACHI 3:10

COMMIT YOURSELF

A decision to commit is only a commitment to decide.

We all make a hundred decisions a day, but our commitments are few and far between. That's because it's much harder to commit to do something than it is to decide to do something. Take your relationship with God as an example. At some point in your life you probably made a decision to follow Christ, the doorway to God. Great decision! But until you committed yourself to Christ, your decision probably didn't lead to any changes in your life. Deciding to follow Christ is acknowledging that He needs to take control of your life and change you from the inside out. Committing to Christ means you actually give Him that control. You become a *fully devoted follower of Christ.*

The essence of being a fully devoted follower of Christ is to turn your decision into a commitment by surrendering control of your life to Him.

"So no one can become my disciple without
giving up everything for me."

LUKE 14:33

No Limits

The love of God has no limits.

Human love is conditional. Whether we're dealing with a friendship or a marriage, our commitments will only go so far. Friendships fail and marriages end in divorce because one can no longer tolerate the other.

But God's love is unconditional. He loved us before we were even interested in Him. He continues to love us even as we disappoint Him with our immature attitudes. And His love for us prevails although our conduct may offend Him. There is nothing we could do that would make God love us less.

God's love extends to us in full measure. It is not distributed in small portions as we earn "spiritual brownie points" if we are good deed doers. There is nothing we can do to make God love us more.

God loves us unconditionally even though He knows we can't love Him back to that extent. That's what makes His love so perfect.

Whether we are high above the sky or in the deepest ocean, nothing in all creation will ever be able to separate us from the love of God that is revealed in Christ Jesus our Lord.

ROMANS 8:39

GOD'S DAY

In the Old Testament, the Sabbath simply referred to the seventh day of the week. This was an important observance, because "God blessed the seventh day and declared it holy, because it was the day when he rested from his work of creation" (Gen. 2:3). Whether we observe the Sabbath on Saturday or Sunday, God wants us to set aside one day a week for Him by resting from our routine and work. Unfortunately, most of us are just as busy on God's day as we are the rest of the week.

May we suggest a new approach—God's approach—to His day? Set it apart for God. Celebrate His involvement in the big and small stuff in your life. Going to church is a good start, but don't rely on your pastor to celebrate for you. Continue to rest in God at home by recalling His faithfulness and enjoying His goodness.

"Remember to observe the Sabbath day by keeping it holy."

WORRIES

Worries are like warts: Each of them grows on you;
neither serves any beneficial purpose,
and you should get rid of both of them.

What should you do when it seems as though your worries are consuming you—when the events of your life are controlling you instead of the other way around? What should you do to gain a proper perspective on your life?

Consider the obstacles that Jesus faced in His life. Opposition was everywhere. Everyone wanted a piece of His time. No one really understood Him. Nonetheless, Jesus never lost His perspective. He didn't worry about the course of events in His life. Jesus knew that His heavenly Father was in control.

Worries can be a burdensome weight on your life if you carry them around with you. But it is foolish to do so (and utterly unnecessary). Worrying doesn't accomplish anything. Instead of fretting, spend your mental energy trusting God to work things out. Jesus let His Father be in control, and so should you.

"So I tell you, don't worry about everyday life—
whether you have enough food, drink, and clothes."
MATTHEW 6:25

LAUGH IT UP

Laugh at yourself as much as others do.

Nobody likes a sore loser, but more than that, nobody likes someone who can't laugh at himself. We're not talking about laughing at your own jokes (which is also annoying). No, if you can't laugh at yourself, we suspect that one or more of the following conditions exist:

You don't consider yourself to be funny. Now, this can't be true. Everybody has at least a little sense of humor.

You don't like people laughing at you. What do you expect them to do? Because you aren't laughing, they have to laugh *at* you rather than *with* you.

You take yourself way too seriously. Here's the real reason.

Our advice is to lighten up and enjoy life. You might even ask God to put a little laughter on your lips and humor in your heart.

He will. . .
fill your mouth with laughter
and your lips with shouts of joy.

THE DEPTHS OF JOY

Enjoy happiness; treasure joy.

Happiness is a pretty hot commodity these days. Ask someone what he wants out of life, and chances are he will say, "I just want to be happy." Happiness is okay, and it's nice to have, but we need to understand that happiness comes and goes because it's dependent on our emotions. If we feel good, we're happy. Simple as that. When people say, "I just want to be happy," they are really saying, "I just want to feel good all the time."

News flash! Life isn't like that. Life is ups and downs and emotions all over the place. No one can feel good all the time. That's why we need to seek joy rather than happiness. Happiness is on the surface, joy is deep. Happiness is temporary, joy abides. Happiness comes from the things of this world, joy comes from God.

Always be full of joy in the Lord.
I say it again—rejoice!
PHILIPPIANS 4:4

Teenagers quickly learn that it is easier to ask forgiveness than to ask permission. If they ask for permission first, their request may be denied. So they go ahead and do what they want, and they are later prepared to say: "I'm sorry. I didn't know I shouldn't have done that."

If we are honest with ourselves, we often take the same approach with God. We make our plans for what we want, and we leave God totally out of the planning process. After all of the choices have been made, then we involve God by asking Him to "bless" what we have already decided to do.

Don't treat God like a magic wand that you wave over your plans. Involve Him in the decisions of your life at the very beginning. Let Him direct you (instead of the other way around).

Trust in the Lord with all your heart;
do not depend on your own understanding.
Seek his will in all you do, and he will direct your paths.

LITTLE THINGS HURT THE MOST

Anger is one of the few things that gets everyone's attention.

Not only do you please God when you control your anger, but you prevent the devil from using your anger to his advantage. Think of it! In one fell swoop of thoughtful control, you can please God and deny the devil. Talk about your two-for-one deal!

Keep in mind that the devil doesn't need your rage to do his dirty work. It's the little things that do the most damage: sarcastic comments, cutting remarks, backbiting, undermining, and lying—all of which you can do with a smile on your face and anger in your heart.

This is the kind of anger that is the most destructive, because it's out before you know it, or worse, without your even noticing. But others notice, and so do God and the devil. So keep a lid on your anger, or deal with it as soon as you are aware of what you've done.

Don't let the sun go down while you are still angry,
for anger gives a mighty foothold to the Devil.
EPHESIANS 4:26–27

THE POWER OF WORDS

We create many of our own problems,
and most of those are the result of careless conversation.

S*ticks and stones may break my bones, but words can* *never hurt me.* We teach that to children so they won't take hurtful words seriously, but that just isn't possible. More than any other force on Earth, words can hurt, discourage, depress, and even destroy others.

What we need to do is teach our children to use words to encourage rather than discourage. James understood that the tongue is capable of doing "enormous damage" (James 3:5). Of course, the tongue itself isn't responsible for what it says. It merely expresses the thoughts in our minds and the feelings in our hearts.

A careful tongue is a tongue in control, especially when it comes to the small stuff—those casual comments, those words spoken "under our breath"—that so easily slip out and so quickly do damage. So teach your children well, and listen to your own advice.

We all make many mistakes,
but those who control their tongues can also
control themselves in every other way.

JAMES 3:2

YOUR FAMILY

In a hospitable home,
everyone serves each other because each one considers
the others to be very special people.

Hospitality is often defined as the display of thoughtfulness to strangers and guests. But having guests over for dinner is only part of hospitality—the easy part. The more challenging aspect of hospitality happens after the door shuts when the visitors leave: Can your family treat each other with the same attention and respect that is reserved for special visitors?

We are often more kind to strangers and friends than we are to the members of our family. The "outsiders" get the best part of us, while the people in our own household get the worst part of us. There's an old saying that goes, "Familiarity breeds contempt," but it doesn't have to be true just because it is old.

Here's another old saying: "I command you to love each other" (John 15:17). When Jesus said these words, He didn't exclude those with whom you share a bathroom and refrigerator.

Dear friends,
let us continue to love one another, for love comes from God.
1 JOHN 4:7

ARE YOU DEVOTED?

It's easy to focus on your devotions rather than the object of your devotions. As you go through this book (or your own Bible study routine), do your best to focus on God rather than the discipline of daily devotions. If you focus on the devotions, your routine can easily become mundane, kind of like a homework assignment. But if you focus on God, then you will learn what it means to be devoted instead of just having devotions.

Being devoted simply means giving our time, our effort, our money, and ourselves to someone, some purpose, or some thing. We can be devoted to a career, a person, or even a hobby or activity. So why not devote ourselves to God? Let's meet with Him daily to get to know Him better, to learn what pleases Him, and to find out what He wants us to do.

"Get to know the God of your ancestors.
Worship and serve him with your whole heart
and with a willing mind."

GOD'S WILL

*Remember that God's will is not
so much a function of time and place
as it is an attitude of the heart.*

People make God's will harder than it needs to be. It is *not* primarily a device for deciding details. (Where do I live? What college do I choose? Whom do I marry? Should I drink Pepsi or Coke?) God's will is more about finding out more about God.

Jesus simply summed up God's will for your life when He said: "And you must love the Lord your God with all your heart, all your soul, all your mind, and all your strength. . . . [and] love your neighbor as yourself" (Mark 12:30–31). That's it. No secret formula. No list of "pros and cons." Just staying focused on God.

The details and decisions of your life will fall into place if your heart is in the right place—and that's what "God's will" is all about.

---

*For God is working in you,
giving you the desire to obey him
and the power to do what pleases him.*
PHILIPPIANS 2:13

PRAY EARNESTLY

If you want to hear from God, read the Bible;
if you want God to hear you, pray.

There's a reason why God wants us to devote ourselves to prayer—it works. God doesn't ask us to do stuff for His own amusement. That would make Him more like a heavenly drill sergeant, who barks, "Drop and give me twenty!" just to show us who's boss.

God isn't our drill sergeant, and He isn't our boss. He's our loving heavenly Father Who wants us to succeed as we relate to Him and others. He's even given us a success manual (the Bible) so we'll know how to get along in this world and prepare for the next. And He's given us prayer so we can tell Him our deepest needs.

Prayer is so much more than reciting words. It's talking with God about everything in your life, from the small stuff to your big concerns. And when you pray earnestly, God promises to answer in ways that will amaze you.

"I will answer them before they even call to me.
While they are still talking to me about their needs,
I will go ahead and answer their prayers!"
ISAIAH 65:24

GENEROSITY

"Giving until it hurts" isn't an accurate measure of generosity because some people are more easily hurt than others.

Most people consider themselves to be generous. But true generosity requires more than just plunking a few coins into the Salvation Army bucket at Christmastime. Ask yourself these questions:

1. Do I have the proper attitude? God wants you to be a cheerful giver (2 Cor. 9:7). How much you give away is irrelevant if your motive isn't right.

2. Is my generosity productive? A contribution to "Citizens Against Speed Bumps" may be tax deductible, but is it a worthy investment of God's resources? Your giving should make a difference in the lives of people in need.

Let God lead your decisions for where and how much to give.

Tell them to use their money to do good.
They should be rich in good works
and should give generously to those in need,
always being ready to share with others
whatever God has given them.
1 TIMOTHY 6:18

CIRCUMSTANCES

Do you feel like the circumstances in your life are out of control? Do you find yourself in situations that are just the opposite of what was on your agenda? Are you frustrated that things are not turning out according to your plan?

Much of what happens in your life is beyond your control. Sometimes it is as insignificant as an unexpected change in the weather that ruins your weekend plans; other times it may be catastrophic, such as a terminal illness. You have no choice in these circumstances, but you can choose how you will respond to these situations.

Instead of being infuriated by your own inability to alter these events, be thankful that God is all-powerful and has control over all of these things. He can either change the circumstances, or He can give you the strength to endure them.

I have learned the secret of living in every situation,
whether it is with a full stomach or empty, with plenty or little.
For I can do everything with the help of Christ
who gives me the strength I need.

Developing the Right Habits

It is easier to form good habits than to break bad ones.

God can give you the ability and power to change the way you live. With His help, you can choose to stop living your life in a nonstop pattern of sin.

The best way to stop—or at least slow down—the sin pattern that comes so naturally for you is by developing new habits. The old habits can be broken while the new ones are being established.

Developing new habits doesn't come automatically. First, you must identify the conduct in your life that needs to stop. Next, you need to learn from God's Word the type of lifestyle that God wants you to have. Then, you need to implement the new pattern of living—repeating it constantly so that it becomes an automatic habit.

You can't accomplish all of this on your own. But you don't have to because God is anxious to help you.

---

*So now we can tell who are children of God
and who are children of the Devil.
Anyone who does not obey God's commands and
does not love other Christians does not belong to God.*
1 John 3:10

LOVING GOD

When we respond to God's help and ask Him to save us and realize that God does just that—even though we don't deserve it—we can have a variety of emotions: gratitude, relief, amazement, and joy. But the greatest emotion—and the only one God asks us to have in response to His love and grace—is love.

We should be thankful and joyful in our Christian lives, but those emotions aren't that hard to come by when we see God working in the small stuff of our lives. Loving God, however, takes effort and sacrifice. It doesn't flow naturally. That's why God commands us to do it.

This isn't emotional love, but love that understands and truly wants the best for the other person. When you want the best for God, you give your best to God. You consciously and willfully love God with all that is in you.

"And you must love the LORD your God
with all your heart,
all your soul, and all your strength."

DEUTERONOMY 6:5

GLOWING IN THE NIGHT

Display what you believe by how you behave.

You've heard of a stealth bomber, but how about a stealth Christian? Here's a guy who figures that once he's saved, there's nothing else to do. He tries to blend quietly into society so that no one will notice the radical ideas Christians are sometimes known for. A stealth Christian thinks nothing of adopting some of the "harmless" habits and ways of the world. After all, God is a forgiving God, right? We've been saved by grace, not by works, so what's the big deal?

There are two problems with this strategy. First, "you can't ignore God and get away with it. You will always reap what you sow!" (Gal. 6:7). Second, God doesn't want His children to fly under the radar. He wants us to be "the light of the world—like a city on a mountain, glowing in the night for all to see" (Matt. 5:14). This is what God wants because this is what people need.

"Don't hide your light under a basket! Instead, put it on a stand and let it shine for all."
MATTHEW 5:15

THE WORTH OF THE WORD

The Bible has absolutely no effect on a lot of people. This isn't the fault of the Bible. The problem is with the people who neglect to read it.

To be effective, your Bible must serve a greater purpose than as a decoration for your bookcase, as a dust-collector on your nightstand, or as a paperweight on your desk. It must be opened. It must be read. And it must be studied.

You wouldn't let an important letter sit in your mailbox without being opened. And you wouldn't ignore an E-mail from an influential person. The content of those items would be too significant to ignore. So don't neglect the personal message that God has waiting for you in His Word. What He has to say to you will change your life (but only if you read it).

Your word is a lamp for my feet
and a light for my path.

ANGELS ALL AROUND

Appreciate angels but don't worship them.

Angels are all around us in two different ways. First, you can't help but notice them in your local gift shops and museums. Images of angels are displayed on coffee mugs and portrayed in paintings. In our popular culture, angels have become a sort of good luck charm, which is a false image of angels.

The other ways angels are around us are in the real sense. Angels are very real spirit beings created by God for a single purpose: to serve and worship God. Now, God has done an amazing thing by ordering His angels to protect us, but we should never put angels on a pedestal (or on the head of a pin, for that matter). We should not worship angels (Col. 2:18). What we should do is worship and thank God for sending His angels to help and protect us, even when we don't realize it.

For he orders his angels to protect you wherever you go.
They will hold you with their hands to keep you
from striking your foot on a stone.
PSALM 91:11–12

RESPONDING TO GOD

When God speaks, listen; when God commands, obey;
when God leads, follow.

Think about this. God loves us, and He knows what is best for us, so He wants us to follow His precepts. But He won't force us to do so. He could have made us like robots that would automatically follow His directions. But He didn't. God gave us a free will, and we can decide for ourselves whether we will obey His commandments and follow His divine principles.

You shouldn't have to pop a cranial corpuscle to decide whether you should follow God's plan for your life. Let's see. . . He knows everything (that's a good start), He loves you (so He's got your best interest in mind), and He is wholly holy (so there is no risk of Him being devious with His advice). Those seem like pretty good credentials, don't they?

"Anyone who listens to my teaching and obeys me is wise,
like a person who builds a house on solid rock.
Though the rain comes in torrents and the floodwaters rise
and the winds beat against that house,
it won't collapse, because it is built on rock."
MATTHEW 7:24–25

WORKING TOGETHER

*Beautiful music is achieved not because
the entire orchestra plays the same instrument,
but because the different instruments are
playing the same tune in the same key.*

An interesting thing happens when people in a group work *against* each other rather than *with* each other: nothing. All of the productivity is slowed (and usually wasted) when people are more concerned about their own interests than the goal of the group. When this happens, hurt feelings and confusion are the result. There is no place where this problem crops up more often than at church.

You are probably involved in several group projects or a few committees at your church. (If you aren't, you should be.) Instead of worrying about your own interests, become aware of how the strengths of others in the group can complement your weaknesses. Realize that God has uniquely equipped you, and each of the others, to carry out His purposes. Each one of you plays a necessary part in accomplishing God's plan. Appreciate those differences.

God has given each of us the ability to do certain things well.
ROMANS 12:6

Here's a question about God that's at the top of everyone's list: How can a loving God allow pain and suffering? That's a legitimate question, and you should be ready to answer it (warning: it's not easy).

God did not create evil or pain or suffering. He created human beings who were perfect and perfectly free to choose or not to choose God. That's the good news. The bad news is that the perfect humans chose evil over God, therefore introducing sin and its consequences into the world (Rom. 5:12). But all was not lost.

God gave us more Good News, this time in the person of Jesus, Who overcame evil and brought us God's forgiveness (Rom. 5:15). He suffered on our behalf and knows what it's like for us to suffer. Jesus is the One Who makes it possible to learn from and ultimately overcome our adversity.

Since he himself has gone through suffering and temptation, he is able to help us when we are being tempted.

THE FINAL CURTAIN?

Death can't be cheated, but it can be defeated.

As much as we'd like to avoid the subject of death, it's hard not to think about it. Is death the final curtain? Or is it possible to cheat death? Is all this business about living forever a bunch of nonsense, or is it the truth? Many people believe there's nothing after death, but the Bible teaches otherwise (Heb. 9:27).

The biggest authority in the world is Jesus. From the time His lifelong friend, John, was beheaded, to the time Jesus was put to death on the cross, Jesus knew death. Yet He also knew that He would ultimately defeat death, and not just for Himself, but for all who believe in Him. When you put your life in Christ, you can be sure that physical death isn't final. Because of His resurrection from the dead, we can defeat death just as Jesus did.

"I am the resurrection and the life.
Those who believe in me,
even though they die like everyone else, will live again.
They are given eternal life for believing in me
and will never perish."
JOHN 11:25–26

GOD IS THINKING ABOUT YOU

God does not let anything in the universe distract Him from thinking about you.

There are many erroneous images of God. Some people think He is a cold and impersonal "force." Others consider God to be like a doddering old man with a long beard (like Charlton Heston as Moses). And those who are enamored with political correctness might consider God to be a woman (or at least a supernatural being that is gender neutral).

The Bible identifies God as our heavenly Father. But don't get the idea that He is a father that is too busy with His work that He doesn't have time for you. You are God's work. You are what He thinks about all day long. Since before the world was created, God knew and loved you.

As you go about your hectic schedule today, take a little time to think about God—because He is thinking about you.

How precious are your thoughts about me, O God!
They are innumerable!
I can't even count them;
they outnumber the grains of sand!
Psalm 139:17-18

CONFUSE YOUR ENEMIES

The best way to confuse your enemies is to love them.

We have a natural tendency to love people who love us, and to hate those who hate us. That may be the way we feel like doing things, but that's not the way we're supposed to respond. As He did so often, Jesus taught something that goes against our natural reactions. We want to get even, settle the score, and stand up for our rights when we've been wronged. We think we deserve the right to retaliate. Jesus calls us to an unusual response in which we show love and forgiveness toward our enemies.

Imagine how you will confuse and confound your enemy when you respond with love and kindness. That type of response may change the heart of your enemy. It will certainly change yours.

Instead, do what the Scriptures say:
"If your enemies are hungry, feed them.
If they are thirsty, give them something to drink,
and they will be ashamed of what they have done to you."
ROMANS 12:20

HOW TO BE SIGNIFICANT

Everyone wants his or her life to count for something, to be meaningful, and to make a difference. What does it take to be significant? Does it take wealth, fame, power, or brilliance? Who do you have to *be* and what can you *do* to make your life really count for something?

Real significance is not a matter of greatness, or fame or influence. True significance is found in serving. Jesus was the most significant person the world has ever known, yet He acted like a servant.

If you want your life to have significance and meaning, then look for ways that you can serve other people.

Then he said,
"Anyone who wants to be the first
must take last place and be the servant of everyone else."

FORGIVENESS IS BIG

Forgiveness opens the door to our relationship with God.

Forgiveness is very big in God's eyes. Very big. Without His forgiveness of our sins, we couldn't get near God because He wouldn't get near us. We should thank God every day for His forgiveness, which opens the door to our relationship with Him.

A lot of us think forgiveness is a one-way street. We become aware of God's forgiveness, accept God's forgiveness through Jesus Christ, and then go about our lives. But God asks more of us. He wants us to forgive others, especially those who have hurt us deeply.

Let's be honest. That's a very tough assignment. We find it very difficult to forgive those who have hurt or offended us. And yet that's exactly why God asks us to do it. Forgiveness is very big in God's eyes, and it needs to be very big in our eyes as well.

You must make allowance for each other's faults and forgive the person who offends you.
COLOSSIANS 3:13

FORGIVENESS IS NOT AN OPTION

God doesn't ask us to do something He hasn't already done for us.

Why do we find it so hard to forgive others? Why do we hold grudges and refuse others the privilege and honor of our forgiveness? We can think of at least one big reason: They have hurt us and consequently don't deserve our forgiveness (at least not for a while). Besides, they haven't asked for our forgiveness. Why should we forgive someone who doesn't want to be forgiven?

Whenever we get stingy with our forgiveness, we need to remember that in our relationship to God, we are the offenders and God is the offended. We have hurt God and don't deserve His forgiveness, yet He didn't wait until we asked Him to forgive us. Out of His deep love for us, He forgave us while we were still in rebellion to Him.

When we are reluctant to forgive others, we must remember that God wants us to.

Remember, the Lord forgave you,
so you must forgive others.
COLOSSIANS 3:13

The Other Side of Forgiveness

God wants us to be less like us and more like Him.

Forgive us our sins, just as we have forgiven those who have sinned against us." Have you ever prayed that prayer? Of course you have, hundreds of times, because it's from The Lord's Prayer (Matt. 6:12). But have you thought about what that means? Does God really forgive us in the same way we forgive others?

God has forgiven us, and He continues to forgive us. He doesn't "constantly accuse us" and "has removed our rebellious acts as far away from us as the east is from the west" (Ps. 103:9, 12). He doesn't keep any records. How unlike us! Yet that's what God wants us to be—unlike ourselves and more like Him. As we forgive others, we don't necessarily trigger God's forgiveness for us, but we show Him that His forgiveness is real in our lives. Whenever we ask God to forgive us, we should make sure we have forgiven the people who have offended us.

---

*"If you forgive those who sin against you,
your heavenly Father will forgive you."*
MATTHEW 6:14

HOLINESS

You can't get holy in a hurry.

Actually, you *can* get holy in a hurry. It happens immediately when you turn your life over to God. At that moment, because Christ paid the penalty for your sins, God sees you as righteous. Your sins (past and future) are gone. This is *positional* holiness—how God sees you.

But when we say "You can't get holy in a hurry," we're talking about *practical* holiness—the actions and attitudes in your life. Even when you allow God to direct your life, you will still be tempted to act according to your old nature. All of your old undesirable habits and thoughts won't immediately vanish.

While positional holiness happens immediately, practical holiness happens gradually as you align your thinking with God's precepts. As your thoughts change, your conduct will change. You'll find increasing evidences of holiness in your life as you remain diligent in your devotion to God.

But now you must be holy in everything you do, just as God— who chose you to be his children—is holy.

1 PETER 1:15

YOU AREN'T STUCK WITH "PLAN B"

*The only reason God hates divorce is
because of what it does to us.*

For many people, divorce has occurred in their lives. Are they doomed to experience less than a good life because of their failed marriage? Are they stuck with living in an inferior "Plan B" world because God doesn't like what they have done?

God does not reserve His love only for those who follow His intended "Plan A" (and aren't we glad of that, because every one of us has stepped outside of God's "Plan A" for our lives in different areas). We have a God Who is in the business of restoring relationships. God may hate divorce because of how it tears apart what He has put together (Mal. 2:16), but He is always ready to forgive and receive us back into fellowship with Him. He never abandons us. He never quits on us. He never gives up on us.

---

*"Since they are no longer two but one,
let no one separate them,
for God has joined them together."*
MATTHEW 19:6

DECEIT

Deceit is like potato chips. It's difficult to stop at the average.

The cable networks are filled with infomercials that promote healthy living with diet programs, exercise equipment, or greaseless cookware. All that paraphernalia won't help much if you are living a deceitful life.

Dishonesty is very detrimental to your health. When you live a long time with deceit, it begins to take its toll on your body and your mind. You become frantic and depressed as you must constantly create more lies in order to cover what you have already said and done. Guilt begins to eat away at you. It's a tough way to live.

On the other hand, when you confess the lies and begin to live in truth—when honesty becomes your policy—you will experience a joy and a level of freedom you never thought possible. The world asks you to lie and suffer the detrimental effects. God asks you to live honestly and enjoy the benefits.

The LORD hates those who don't keep their word,
but he delights in those who do.
Proverbs 12:22

God Won't Tempt You

Never confuse a trial with a temptation.

There's a difference between trials and temptations. A trial is something that happens to us through outer circumstances or our own actions. God allows trials in our lives because they have the potential to make us "partners with Christ in his suffering" (1 Pet. 4:13). On the other hand, a temptation can entice us to do the wrong thing.

God is never tempted to do wrong. Even when Satan tempted Jesus, there was never a possibility that Jesus would make a mistake. He stood on the Word of God and kept Satan and his test at bay.

God doesn't tempt us to do wrong, either. More than likely, our temptations come from "the lure of our own evil desires" (James 1:14). God wants us to endure our temptations through the power of the Holy Spirit, and He will bless us for it (James 1:12).

God is never tempted to do wrong,
and he never tempts anyone else either.
JAMES 1:13

WHY NOT?

Have you ever gotten into a circular discussion with a little kid? Every statement you make is greeted with a "Why?" The first couple of times it happens, it's cute. But after a dozen "Why?" questions to your simple statements, you feel bogged down and you just want to move on. You don't blame the kid for asking "Why?" so much. He's a kid. He doesn't know any better. But when a full-grown adult questions everything people tell him, it can be annoying.

We all need to ask questions to clarify the issues and get information, but when our questions keep us from getting things done, they stop being helpful. At some point you have to stop asking "Why?" and ask "Why not?" If you haven't asked "Why not?" in a while, you may be too complacent.

"I know all the things you do,
that you are neither hot nor cold.
I wish you were one or the other!"

CHOICES, CHOICES

*You won't have to take your chances so often
if you make wise choices more often.*

Choices. We make them every day. Some are insignificant. ("What cereal should I eat for breakfast?") Others are monumental. ("Should I marry this person?")

Behavior is also a matter of choice. Every day, throughout the day, we choose between following the desires of our sinful nature or following the direction of the Holy Spirit. The sinful nature will lead to immorality, destruction, and despair. In sharp contrast, the Holy Spirit will fill your life with love, joy, and peace.

When you are faced with the choice of following your sinful nature or following the Holy Spirit, remind yourself of the consequences of each choice.

---

*Once we, too, were foolish and disobedient. . . .
Our lives were full of evil and envy. . . .
But then God our Savior showed us his kindness and love.
He saved us, not because of the good things we did,
but because of his mercy.*
TITUS 3:3–5

GOD ISN'T LIKE US

Never regret that God is your judge.
He's the fairest judge you'll ever meet.

We make lousy judges. Unlike a real judge, who considers all the evidence, we make snap judgments based on what people look like, what they say, and what they do. How arrogant! Who do we think we are, passing judgment on others by what they do and how they look? No wonder we are so slow to forgive others. If we base our judgments on outer actions and appearances, which people really can't change, when are we going to forgive them?

We can thank God that He isn't like us. God looks beyond appearance to the inner qualities—like faith and character—that make us who we are. His justice and His judging are completely accurate and true, and His forgiveness is totally effective, because He sees the real us. We can trust God to judge us fairly and honestly.

"The LORD doesn't make decisions the way you do!
People judge by outward appearance."
1 SAMUEL 16:7

DEVELOP THE INNER YOU

Painting the outside of a house isn't worth much
if the inside is a mess.

Okay, so there's a downside to God's judgment. Since He is completely fair and honest, and because He sees the real us from the inside out, there's no fooling Him. We can't put on a front, like we do with people, by acting and looking a certain way.

Before we act, God knows what we're thinking. Before we even think about doing something—no matter how small—God is there. That could be more than a little unnerving, but you shouldn't take God that way. He's not a spy. He's not intruding into your private life. God simply knows you completely (and loves you anyway).

So here's what you do. Spend as much time developing the inner you as you do maintaining the outer you. Pay attention to stuff like character and integrity. That's the stuff that counts in God's all-seeing eyes.

"But the LORD looks at
a person's thoughts and intentions."
1 SAMUEL 16:7

GOD'S WORD IS TIMELESS

Spend time in God's Word because its lessons are timeless.

Do you know the most common complaint about physicians? It has nothing to do with their ability. People don't like the outdated magazines in their doctor's office. Nobody likes stale news or outdated stories. Articles quickly become irrelevant in our fast-changing society.

The Bible doesn't have an expiration date. It is timeless. Its description of God is never obsolete because God's nature never changes. He is the same yesterday, today, and forever, so what was written about Him centuries ago by Moses, and King David, and the apostle Paul is still true today.

Oh, the stories of shepherds and life in ancient Palestine may differ from our contemporary cultural experience, but God's plan to connect with the human race through Jesus Christ hasn't changed. The truth and message of the Bible will never be outdated. (Hey, maybe doctors should put copies of the Bible in their waiting rooms.)

Your justice is eternal, and your law is perfectly true.
As pressure and stress bear down on me,
I find joy in your commands.
PSALM 119:142, 143

How Much Is Enough?

You can handle wealth if
you are more concerned about sense than dollars.

How much is enough? Madison Avenue tells you to have the newest, the best, the biggest, and the most. Society seems to judge people by what and how much they own. To avoid the quest to possess, should you deprive yourself of every convenience, or should you take a vow of poverty and give every piece of clothing with a designer label to the missionaries?

Jesus wasn't too concerned about possessions. He was born in a borrowed stable; He fed five thousand people with a borrowed lunch; He was even buried in a borrowed tomb. But don't think that Jesus was setting a pattern that requires you to rent your furniture rather than purchase it.

The question is not whether you rent or own. It is not even *how much* you have. The relevant issue is whether you are depending upon your possessions for your security or your happiness. Are you?

"Real life is not measured by how much we own. . .
Yes, a person is a fool to store up earthly wealth
but not have a rich relationship with God."
Luke 12:15, 21

POWER UP

There are two ways to acquire power:
on the outside or from the inside.
God gives power from the inside.

The way people normally acquire power is on the outside. They work out with a bunch of weights and gain the power of strength. They go to college for a long time and gain the power of knowledge. They work their way to the top of a company and gain the power of prestige. Or they run for political office and gain the power of position. All of these things equal power, but they develop on the outside, and they take many years to acquire.

God doesn't need all of these outward devices to give you power, and He doesn't need a lot of time, either. When you enter into a personal relationship with God through Christ, something very amazing happens: You receive the power of the Holy Spirit, and it happens from the inside. No one is exempt. The Bible says that "we have all received the same Spirit" (1 Cor. 12:13).

"But when the Holy Spirit has come upon you,
you will receive power."

JESUS

SIT STILL

*The time to find moments of stillness and quiet is
when it's the most difficult to do so.*

Have you ever sat behind a young child in church?
After sitting still for a few minutes, the fidgeting begins.
Then the child transitions into the wiggling stage. After a
while, the kid is crawling over the chair like it's a jungle gym.
The parents were hoping that the child would benefit from
being in church, but the child was too busy wriggling to hear
what was being said.

That squirming child can be a metaphor for our lives
with God. We are usually so busy fidgeting with the activities
of life that we miss hearing what God wants to tell us. Even
worthwhile activities that benefit our family, our church, or
our community can distract us from spending time with God.

Stop fidgeting for a few moments each day. Read the
Bible, and listen to what God is saying to you. You'll have difficulty hearing Him unless you sit still.

---

*The LORD is wonderfully good to those who
wait for him and seek him.*
LAMENTATIONS 3:25

JUDGE FAIRLY

Change the way you treat others
before you question the way God treats you.

God knows what poor judges we are, so He asks us not to judge. He also knows we can't help judging others, so He has intensified His request by reminding us that we will be judged according to how we judge others. Ouch. Now He's getting personal.

God has a right to do this, of course, and we have no right to question Him and how He does things (Isa. 55:8). But neither should we think He isn't being fair. God is incapable of being anything but fair. Everything He does is for our own good. In this matter of judging and being judged, what God is essentially asking us to do is put ourselves in the other person's shoes. Just like we don't want to be judged unfairly, we shouldn't judge others unfairly. And if we do, we can expect unfair judgment to come our way.

"Stop judging others, and you will not be judged.
For others will treat you as you treat them."
MATTHEW 7:1–2

WISDOM

*Lots of things come automatically with age,
but wisdom isn't one of them.*

There are two kinds of wisdom: worldly wisdom and spiritual wisdom.

Worldly wisdom involves applying knowledge and human understanding to certain factual situations. This type of wisdom can usually be explained in the context of benefits and detriments. (For example, it is not wise to insult your boss due to the detriment of unemployment.)

Spiritual wisdom doesn't rely on human understanding. In fact, spiritual wisdom refers to a belief system that can be comprehended only through spiritual insight. (For example, those who do not know God cannot understand how it is possible to sense His direction when He can't be seen or heard.)

Worldly wisdom can be obtained through experience and gives you insight into human nature. Spiritual wisdom comes through the Holy Spirit and gives you insight into God's nature.

---

*The wisdom we speak of is the secret wisdom of God. . . .
But we know these things because
God has revealed them to us by his Spirit.*
1 CORINTHIANS 2:7, 10

THE FRIENDSHIP FACTOR

A true friend doesn't ask anything in return.

Everyone wants to enjoy the loyalty, support, and companionship of a friend. Friendship works like a two-way street. You are there for your friends, and they are there for you. But what if you get stuck with a friend who doesn't play by the rules? What about friends who are always around when they need you, but can't be found when you need them?

Jesus defined true friendship when He said: "Love each other in the same way that I love you" (John 15:12). There are no limits to how much energy you should put into a friendship. Ultimate friendship requires that you would be willing to sacrifice your life for your friend. You may never be asked to die for a friend, but there are many other ways you can make personal sacrifices for the benefit of your friends through your time, energy, and resources.

"I command you to love each other
in the same way that I love you.
And here is how to measure it—
the greatest love is shown when
people lay down their lives for their friends."
JOHN 15:12–13

HOW TO PRAY

Prayer without effort will be insincere.
Effort without prayer will be ineffective.

Prayer involves more than just kneeling at a bedside with hands folded and eyes closed. It goes beyond just standing on a mountaintop with arms outstretched and head lifted toward the heavens. While these are great postures for prayer, the images are incomplete.

Prayer involves effort (and we don't just mean the grunting to bend down on your knees or the exertion to climb the mountaintop). Sincere prayer requires a willingness to put some action behind what you are asking from God.

Maybe God intends to use you to accomplish the result you are praying for. After you pray for your family and neighbors, do something tangible to show your love for them. After you pray for those who are sick, do something to help them. After you pray for world peace, show kindness to someone.

Saying "Amen" doesn't end your prayer. It's the signal for your action to begin.

The earnest prayer of a righteous person
has great power and wonderful results.
JAMES 5:16

WHAT MAKES A GOOD SERMON?

The measure of a good sermon is the listener's response,
not the pastor's speech.

How does God talk to you? Through the Bible and the inner voice of the Holy Spirit, sure. But don't forget that God also speaks to you through the sermons that you hear.

Most of us make the mistake of sitting in church like we are members of an *audience*. (We are there to be *entertained* by the musicians and *motivated* by the speaker.) That is the wrong approach. When we worship at church, God is the audience—we are the participants. True worship includes responding to the message that is preached—not just listening—but actually applying what we have heard to our lives.

God is speaking to you through the sermons that you hear. Don't rate the quality of the preacher's performance (like a judge at an ice skating competition—8.6 for technical ability and 9.2 for style). Your role is to hear the message and to respond.

Then [Jesus] said,
"Anyone who is willing to hear
should listen and understand!"
MARK 4:8–9

The Best Kind of Humor

Humor works best when it brings joy to others.

Some of the best quotes in the world are about humor (and they aren't even that funny). Here's a sampling:

"Humor is the shock absorber of life; it helps us take the blows" (Peggy Noonan).

"A good laugh is sunshine in a house" (William Makepeace Thackeray).

"Against the assault of laughter nothing can stand" (Mark Twain).

The Bible doesn't say a lot about humor, but there are plenty of principles regarding joy. Humor for humor's sake is often pointless and sometimes demeaning. When humor brings joy to others, it serves a worthwhile purpose. You give people something rather than taking something away.

When you use humor to bring joy to others, you help relieve them of sorrow (Jer. 31:13) and you refresh them (Philem. 7). Most of all, you connect them with God (Ps. 16:11).

We were filled with laughter,
and we sang for joy.
Psalm 126:2

WHERE IS YOUR AFFECTION?

The love of money can do more to you than dollars can do for you.

Have you noticed the destructive power of greed? Friendships end, marriages break apart, crimes are committed, and people stay away from God—all over what? The love of money. Even though we are aware of its potential dangers, the allure remains.

Remember that money is neutral. It is neither good nor bad. It is the *love* of money that presents the problems. But it seems funny that we should be so enamored with it. It can't buy happiness in this life. And it can't buy eternal life. Money can never get you closer to God, but your attraction to it can keep you away from Him. Make sure your affections are for your Maker, not for your money.

But people who long to be rich fall into temptation
and are trapped by many foolish
and harmful desires that plunge them into ruin and destruction.
For the love of money is at the root of all kinds of evil.
And some people, craving money,
have wandered from the faith
and pierced themselves with many sorrows.
1 TIMOTHY 6:9–10

Begin Your Day with God

You can start your day without God,
but you'll never really get started.

King David was a morning person. He loved to get up early and meet the Lord in prayer and meditation. As a king, David's day was full of appointments, decrees, and official duties. David knew that if he was going to carve out time for God, it had to be in the morning before everyone else grabbed for his time.

You may not be the king of a country, but you are probably the king of the house, king of the hill, or the king of your office. You have appointments to keep, decrees to declare, and duties to perform. Your calendar is no less busy than a full-time monarch. So you have to ask yourself, *If David thought it was a good idea to meet God in the morning, why don't I?* It's not that God isn't available later in the day. He always has time for you. You're the one who gets too busy for God.

Listen to my voice in the morning, LORD.
Each morning I bring my requests to you
and wait expectantly.
PSALM 5:3

REMEMBER YESTERDAY

If you don't remember what God did for you yesterday,
you'll have trouble trusting Him for today.

Another reason for beginning your day with God is that you can better remember what God did for you yesterday. At the end of the day you are either too wound up or too tired to do much reflecting. God has worked in your life in a hundred different ways, but you have no focus when the day is done. Nothing but the biggest circumstances stand out.

If you want to reflect on the small stuff God has accomplished in your life, sit quietly in the early morning with your Bible and your coffee and just reflect. Let God speak to you from His Word, and then close your eyes and let Him bring to mind the wonderful things He did for you yesterday. Soon the little remembrances will dawn on you and wash over you like a sweet scent, and you will realize that God is going to do it all over again today.

Understand, therefore, that the LORD your God is indeed God.
He is the faithful God who keeps his covenant for
a thousand generations and constantly loves those who
love him and obey his commands.
DEUTERONOMY 7:9

BOOST YOUR MEMORY

If you are having a difficult time being thankful,
the problem may be your memory.

You are less likely to say "What has God done for me lately?" and more likely to remember the things God has done for you by memorializing them. Here's what we mean. In the Old Testament, the great leader, Joshua, made it a practice to stack up twelve large stones (one for each of the tribes of Israel) whenever God did something for them. We're not suggesting that you make a rock pile in your front yard to mark a special time when God helped you, but a photograph on the refrigerator might serve as a reminder. Or you might want to keep a special calendar or journal in which you keep track of God's unusual provisions. Whatever you do, make an effort to remember. The more you see what God has done in the past, the more you will see Him at work in the present.

I recall all you have done, O LORD;
I remember your wonderful deeds of long ago.
PSALM 77:11

LEADERSHIP

People will be anxious to serve under a leader
who is willing to serve them.

Lead, follow, or get out of the way" is a rather intimidating phrase implying that only people who are aggressive and bold can lead (while everyone else had better fall into line or stand aside). Is this your idea of leadership? When you are in charge, do you try to intimidate others and order people around?

Modern leadership theory subscribes to the concept of "servant leadership." This was hailed as a groundbreaking management concept in the 1970s. Wow! It only took society a little more than nineteen centuries to catch on to what Jesus taught.

If you want to be an effective leader, be a servant. Forget about the power and prestige and intimidation. Follow the example of Jesus and serve others.

Jesus told them,
"In this world the kings and great men order their people around,
and yet they are called 'friends of the people.'
But among you, those who are the greatest should take
the lowest rank, and the leader should be like a servant."
LUKE 22:25–26

There's Time to Change

It is never too late to make a change in your life.

There are certain stages in life when it is too late. You can't order off the child's menu at the Denny's restaurant after age twelve. You can't get the student discount at the movies after you've graduated. And you can't get hired as an astronaut when you're sixty years old (unless you're John Glenn).

There is no "too late" stage with God. You are never too old to start a personal relationship with Him. And once you have connected with Him, it is never too late to have your life changed by Him.

Now that we think about it, there does come a time when it is too late to respond to God. That would be when your life ends. Death is the ultimate "too late" stage. So, unless you know exactly when that's going to be, you'd better plan on making your changes while you can.

And I am sure that God,
who began the good work within you,
will continue his work until it is finally finished
on that day when Christ Jesus comes back again.
Philippians 1:6

PERSECUTION

*If you aren't being persecuted for your faith,
it may mean that no one can tell that you are a Christian.*

Persecution for your faith can take different forms, and it usually involves suffering in one degree or another. In some countries, Christians are being arrested, beaten, and even murdered for their faith in God. Any persecution you have endured probably hasn't been that severe, but it could still have involved suffering on your part. Even verbal ridiculing can be tough to take.

If you suffer for being a Christian, no matter what the extent, you can rejoice in the fact that it's a privilege. That's right. Rejoice, because when you suffer for claiming the name of Christ, you are being identified with God. It is a privilege to be a child of God, even if you are insulted for it.

*Be happy if you are insulted for being a Christian,
for then the glorious Spirit of God will come upon you.
But it is no shame to suffer for being a Christian.
Praise God for the privilege of being called
by his wonderful name!*
1 PETER 4:14, 16

FAITH ABIDES

Faith is not an emotion.
It is an objective trust placed in a very real God.

Faith is highly underrated. Too many people view faith as some sort of mysterious hocus-pocus. They're too intelligent to have faith. Faith is for children and weak-minded adults. Yet every single day of their lives people have faith in stuff. They believe it's safe to eat their breakfast. They trust the weatherman who says it's not going to rain. They drive on the freeway and have faith that none of the other drivers are going to hit them head-on.

You need faith to live, or else you'd sit at home in the dark and do nothing. Without faith you would die. Believing in God is not for the simple or the weak. It's for thoughtful people who know that without faith, you can't ultimately experience and know God. Faith doesn't come and go. It abides and grows as God reveals Himself more and more to the one who believes.

"And a righteous person will live by faith."
HEBREWS 10:38

LET GOD HAVE A TURN TO TALK

Prayer involves listening to God as well as speaking to Him.

What is your definition of *prayer?*" The most common response to that question is "Talking to God." Unfortunately, that answer is wrong. The correct answer is "Talking *with* God."

Perhaps you think we are being too nitpicky. But there is a huge difference between talking *to* God and talking *with* God. Think about it. Conversation, by its definition, requires two-way communication. Otherwise, it's just one person giving a speech rather than two people conversing.

Maybe you're thinking that prayers have to be one-way only (you to God) because God never replies. Well, He does. But you have to give Him a turn to talk. The next time you pray, don't walk away until you have given God a chance to respond. The Holy Spirit wants to say something to you, but He won't interrupt when you are talking, so you'll have to stop talking and listen.

"The Maker of the heavens and earth—
the LORD is his name—says this:
Ask me and I will tell you some remarkable secrets
about what is going to happen here."
JEREMIAH 33:2-3

DELIGHT IN SEEKING GOD

Seek God. Trust God. Enjoy God.

One of the greatest pleasures in life is seeking God. Many people spend their time avoiding God (sometimes they spend a lifetime), because they think that God is like a warden who wants to imprison them and take away their privileges. Even Christians who have found God try to avoid Him sometimes.

The truth is, we're miserable when we run from God, because without God all we have are our puny pleasures. When we seek God at any level—whether skeptically or wholeheartedly—we eventually discover someone who wants to give us abundant life (John 10:10).

Don't make the mistake of seeking God for temporary solutions to your problems. He can do anything, but He delights in giving you long-lasting peace of mind and heart, and joy unlike anything you can experience on your own.

"If you look for me in earnest,
you will find me when you seek me."
JEREMIAH 29:13

SUCCESS

Before you climb the ladder of success,
be sure to check that it's leaning against the right wall.

Most people evaluate success in terms of what they can accumulate during their lifetime. But that is not God's perspective on success. From a spiritual viewpoint, success is determined by the ultimate destiny of your soul. After all, your life on Earth is only for a fleeting moment compared to eternity.

When Jesus was discussing this subject with the disciples, He explained success in these terms: "And how do you benefit if you gain the whole world but lose your own soul?" (Matt. 16:26).

If you really want to have success that matters and will last forever, then you must be willing to abandon the things of the world and invest your energies in spiritual matters.

"If any of you wants to be my follower,
you must put aside your selfish ambition,
shoulder your cross, and follow me.
If you try to keep your life for yourself, you will lose it.
But if you give up your life for me, you will find true life."
MATTHEW 16:24–25

BE A GOD PLEASER

*You can't please God without adding
a great deal of joy to your life.*

Doing things for others is very rewarding. It's fun to make others happy, to surprise them in some way with a gift or an offer to do something special for them. The more you like someone, the more you try to please them in some way, usually without being asked. In fact, knowing someone well is the key to pleasing them well.

God enjoys our efforts to please Him. Because He's God and He already loves us as much as He can, you can't say that God loves us any more or feels better about us when we please Him. But He does respond when we do the things that please Him.

Of course, the one who is happiest is the one who does the things that please God. Doesn't it make sense, then, that we should discover what those things are?

Try to find out what is pleasing to the Lord.
EPHESIANS 5:10

The Beauty of Creation

When you see a beautiful painting, you compliment the artist.
So, when you experience the beauty in nature, praise the Creator.

Our world is filled with beauty, but usually we are too busy to notice. An early morning routine forces us to miss the sunrise, and we're engulfed with activities into the evening so we don't enjoy the sunset. Maybe your daily commute takes you past majestic scenery—but you never notice because you're too upset by the driver that cut in front of you.

Imagine that you attended an art exhibition featuring incredible paintings by a local artist. If you blasted through the gallery without looking at the paintings, you would insult the artist, and you would be depriving yourself of the beauty on display.

And so it is with the world around you. God is the Master Artist Who creatively designed the beauty in nature. Don't rush through His gallery. Stop long enough to enjoy the splendor of the earth. And compliment Him on His artistry.

The heavens tell of the glory of God.
The skies display his marvelous craftsmanship.
PSALM 19:1

MORE THAN MERE INTEREST

It may be hard to believe in God,
but it is harder not to believe in Him.

There's a difference between merely being *interested* in God and truly *believing* in Him. Those who are just inquisitive don't have any reason to live a godly life; but someone who actually believes in God should have a lifestyle that is consistent with that belief.

Lots of people have a curiosity about God, but they say that they won't believe in Him until they have proof of His existence. That's a stall tactic. The world has all the information about God that is required for belief. The Bible gives the historical facts, and Christians are the living proof. Seeing is not required for believing, because there is sufficient evidence for anyone who is sincerely seeking to find God.

Make sure that you aren't guilty of having mere *interest* instead of true *belief*. (Your lifestyle is an indicator.) The difference will have eternal significance for you.

"Blessed are those who haven't seen me
and believe anyway."
JOHN 20:29

BE A SERVANT

Serving others is the most noble of human endeavors.

God's Kingdom is unlike man's kingdoms and governments. In those organizations, the leaders establish their greatness by exercising authority over their subjects. Those leaders want to be served and honored by those beneath them in the organization.

That's not the way it is in the Kingdom of God. Christianity is based on service to others, so Christian leaders must be interested in serving rather than being served. Our example is Jesus Christ. He did not come to Earth to be served by others, but to serve (Phil. 2:7). He came to offer His life as a sacrifice for our sins. You may never be asked to give your life for someone else, but that attitude of self-sacrificing service should be the mark of your Christianity.

"But among you it should be quite different.
Whoever wants to be a leader among you
must be your servant."
MATTHEW 20:26

WORTH THE EFFORT

You don't need athletic ability to run the Christian race
(but it helps to have a strong heart).

When an athlete steps up on the award platform to receive the gold medal, there is no regret about the hours of hard work spent in training. Winning the prize makes all of the self-discipline worthwhile. The same is true of the Christian life—just like an athlete who adheres to a strict fitness and diet program, a Christian must stay away from people and places that would be detrimental to living a life that honors God.

Of course, there is much more to motivate a Christian than a gold medal. In an athletic competition, only one person wins the gold medal. But every Christian wins, and not just at the end of the "race" when you'll meet Jesus in heaven. The training program for Christianity (prayer, Bible reading, fellowship with other Christians) can bring you closer to God on a daily basis, and that prize makes the self-discipline worthwhile.

***

Remember that in a race everyone runs,
but only one person gets the prize.
You also must run in such a way that you will win.
1 CORINTHIANS 9:24

A Mother's Love

Call your mother—you know how she worries.

It takes so little to make your mother happy. Now your dad is a different story. He is concerned for your future, so he wants to make sure you learn how to mow the lawn, hit a baseball, get good grades, go to a quality university, and land a high-paying job. That's what makes him happy. But your mother? She loves you for who you are. You are the fruit of her womb, the apple of her eye, the crown of her head. "Such a good boy," she'll tell you as she cups your face in her hands. "Such a sweet girl," she'll say as she embraces you.

God created fathers to teach us, but God gave us mothers to love us. All she needs from you is a word, a note, or a call, telling her that you love her and that you wouldn't be where you are without her.

May she who gave you birth be happy.
PROVERBS 23:25

WORDS OF THE HEART

If you want to know what's in your heart,
listen to your mouth.

No one wants to admit being hypocritical, but most of us suffer from that malady from time to time. We often put on a façade of being spiritual, but it is just a show. If we do this too long and too often, we begin to fool ourselves into thinking we are spiritual when we really aren't. How can you tell what's really in your heart?

There is a way to check your true spiritual condition, but it doesn't involve looking at your heart. That's too subjective. Instead of looking at your heart, start your examination about ten inches higher. Listen to the words that come out of your mouth. If you hear lying, gossip, criticism, or bitterness, then you have a serious heart problem. But if you're speaking words of truth, kindness, and encouragement, then your heart is in great spiritual shape.

"Whatever is in your heart determines what you say."
LUKE 6:45

THE PEACE OF GOD

The peace of God is the greatest feeling in the world.

The peace of God is a gift. Jesus said so Himself (John 14:27). The peace of God is a gift because there's no way we can generate it on our own. The world can't give us this kind of peace, either. All the world can do is provide a temporary diversion from our worries and troubles by substituting something else.

The peace of God permeates every part of our being. When we give God our burdens rather than worrying about them, He removes our anxiety. When we give God our doubts and fears, He replaces them with confidence. When we trust God, obey God, and depend on God in all things both big and small, He gives us His gift of peace. The peace of God is a gift, but we have to ask for it.

If you do this, you will experience God's peace,
which is far more wonderful than
the human mind can understand.
PHILIPPIANS 4:7

PRACTICAL PEACE

*You will experience peace when you invite God into
the details of your life.*

The opposite of peace is war, and that's exactly what happens in our lives when God's peace is missing. It isn't an external war, but a war within us, caused by a combination of sin, fear, doubt, and anxiety. We lump all of that stuff together and call it stress, but it's a little more complicated than that.

We try to manage all these negative forces by controlling the details of our lives. "Don't worry, I can handle it," we tell people, but secretly we know our insides are in a knot. None of this is a secret to God. He's completely aware of all the details. He's just waiting for us to ask Him to handle them for us. He won't intrude; we must invite Him. When we do, He'll come to our rescue. When our problems are beyond our ability, He'll give us His ability—and His peace.

---

*His peace will guard your hearts and minds as
you live in Christ Jesus.*
PHILIPPIANS 4:7

PEACE WITH GOD

*The greatest thing about God's peace is
that it gives us peace with Him.*

When we talk about peace and war, we can talk about external battles and internal battles, but there is one more battle we can't ignore: our battle with God. "But wait a minute! I've got nothing against God. I mind my own business, and I expect Him to do the same."

Sorry, it doesn't work that way. While it's true that God won't invade our lives unless we invite Him, our relationship with Him isn't neutral. The Bible says that we are God's enemies because we are sinners (Rom. 5:10). We are at war with God (and that's a battle we can't win).

The only way to end the war with God is to raise the white flag of surrender. We have to accept God's terms for peace, which center on the person and work of Jesus. When we do that, we experience the ultimate peace there is—peace with God.

*Therefore, since we have been made right in God's sight by faith,
we have peace with God because of what
Jesus Christ our Lord has done for us.*
ROMANS 5:1

MARRIAGE

Marriages may be made in heaven,
but they must be lived here on Earth.

Marriage is not to be taken lightly. God designed it to be a sacred union between a man and a woman. It is not just for a moment; it is for a lifetime.

Marriage is in God's plan for some, and it may not be His plan for others. To whatever situation God calls you, it is His gift to you. Remember that God knows what is best for you.

If you are married, then God wants you wholeheartedly devoted to your spouse in love, loyalty, and respect. If you are single, your life should be marked by sexual and moral purity. In either circumstance, God wants your life to reflect His holiness.

As the Scriptures say,
"A man leaves his father and mother and is joined to his wife,
and the two are united into one."
This is a great mystery,
but it is an illustration of the way
Christ and the church are one.
EPHESIANS 5:31–32

PRAYER WORKS

There is no such thing as an unsuccessful prayer.

Do you feel like your prayers are ineffective? Does it seem like they hit the ceiling and don't reach heaven? Is praying an exercise in futility for you?

Don't evaluate the effectiveness of your prayers solely on the basis of whether God gives you what you asked for. (He is not a celestial vending machine.) Sometimes He may respond in the way you asked; other times He may deny your request because it is not in your best interests; or, He may postpone action for reasons that are unknown to you. Regardless of His response, God hears your prayers and attends to them.

Prayer is not designed to give you everything you want. (God is not Santa, and prayers are not your Christmas gift list.) The purpose of prayer is to connect you with God. Every prayer is successful because it links you with God in a personal conversation.

Don't worry about anything; instead,
pray about everything.
Tell God what you need,
and thank him for all he has done.
PHILIPPIANS 4:6

Thinking and Doing

*It's one thing to know what's right,
and another thing entirely to do it.*

Following God requires thinking and doing. You have to know what is right (this involves your *thinking*) and you must put that knowledge into action (this involves *doing*). You can't be a devoted follower of God if you have one aspect without the other. If you intellectually know what is right but fail to act on that knowledge, your life will be ineffective. If you plunge ahead into action but don't have an understanding of God's truth, then your efforts will be misguided. It takes both knowledge and action to pursue God's principles.

God equips you in both of these areas. He has given us His Word—the Bible—so we know what is right and wrong. And He has given us the Holy Spirit to empower our actions.

Following God is not an event. It's a process. Learn what God wants you to do, and then do it.

---

*Solid food is for those who are mature,
who have trained themselves to recognize
the difference between right
and wrong and then do what is right.*
HEBREWS 5:14

The God Who Is

*You begin to seek God for Who He is when
you stop seeking Him for what He can do for you.*

A lot of people think God is Santa Claus. He's the jolly guy with the white beard watching them from heaven to see if they've been naughty or nice. Instead of making their Christmas wish list, however, they pray to God when they need stuff, usually during a time of crisis. They see God as a powerful, almost mythical deity, and their relationship (if you can call it that) is based on what they hope He will do for them.

People with this view of God have very little idea of Who God really is—the God Who loves them and Who wants very much to have a personal relationship with them. The only way to change this view is to seek God for Who He is. Patrick Morley wrote, "There is the God we want, and there is the God Who is, and they are not the same God." Seek the God Who is.

*He prayed,
"O LORD, God of Israel,
there is no God like you in all of heaven and earth."*

With God's Help

God does not help us because we deserve it;
He helps us because He loves us.

If God waited to help us until we deserved it, we would be in big trouble. The cold, hard fact of the matter is that not one single person has ever deserved God's help. Hey, this isn't us talking. The Bible is very clear about this (Rom. 3:12). Besides that, no one is asking for God's help (Rom. 3:11).

Wait a minute. People ask God for help all the time, don't they? Not really. They ask for physical stuff, they ask for health, and they ask for help when they're in trouble, but they don't ask for help where they really need it—in their spiritual lives. That's where we all need God, Who is the only One Who can help us spiritually.

The good news is that God helps us despite ourselves. And He helps us, not because of us, but because of Him. God helps us because it's in His nature to help. He helps us because He loves us.

"You keep your promises and show unfailing love
to all who obey you and are eager to do your will."
2 Chronicles 6:14

CONNECTING WITH GOD

Christ's superiority is the cure for your inferiority.

Do you ever feel as if you're not good enough to please God? That's understandable, because you aren't. But Jesus is, and He can be our connection to God.

Jesus was fully confident that His actions were always pleasing to His heavenly Father. We can never come close to the standard of perfection, but we can use it to our advantage. When we believe in Christ, His righteousness is attributed to us.

Don't let your feelings of inferiority drag you down. Celebrate the fact that, despite your faults, you can belong to God because Christ provides the perfection that you need.

"You are of this world; I am not.
That is why I said that you will die in your sins;
for unless you believe that I am who I say I am,
you will die in your sins.
And the one who sent me is with me—
he has not deserted me.
For I always do those things that are pleasing to him."
JOHN 8:23–24, 29

DON'T PUT GOD IN A BOX

Rather than using God to solve your problems,
use your problems to get closer to God.

God is the world's greatest problem solver, but as long as you see God only in this role, there's going to be a distance between you. Do you feel close to God? Does your life have meaning and purpose? If it doesn't, then perhaps you've put God in a box. You keep Him around for those times when you need Him to help you out of a jam. But when things are going well, you keep Him in your little box and get along quite well all by yourself. Or so you think.

God is much more than a problem solver. He is the eternal, holy, unchangeable, loving, all-powerful, all-knowing God of the universe. He has rescued you from the pit and set your feet on higher ground. He wants to do more than solve your problems. God wants to give you direction and purpose every day of your life.

For who is God except the LORD?
Who but our God is a solid rock?
PSALM 18:31

NATURE'S THEOLOGY

You can learn a great deal about God by studying His creation.

You don't have to attend seminary to gain insights into God's character. You need only to walk outdoors and look up—or look down. Whether you are gazing up at the stars in the midnight sky or looking down at ants parading along a crack in the sidewalk, you can learn about God.

Nature reveals the enormity and power of God. It also reveals His creativity and attention to detail. The fact that our earth is specifically designed to meet the needs of the human race—the air, the light, the food, the climate—tells us that God is interested in us and cares for us.

Learn about God as you observe Him in nature.

From the time the world was created,
people have seen the earth
and sky and all that God made.
ROMANS 1:20

SETTLE FOR THE BEST

*When you feel like settling for less than the best,
think about what God wants for you.*

There will come a day when you realize that God
wants more for you than you could possibly want for yourself.
Maybe you've come to that day already, but if not, here's what
will happen. As you focus on God daily by reading His Word
and talking with Him through prayer, you are going to gain a
greater appreciation for Who God is and what His will is for
you each day. You will recall what God has done in every
detail of your life as you eagerly learn how God wants to build
your character and use you to impact the lives of others.

At that point you will realize that God doesn't just
want you to "get by" each day. He wants you to live your life
fully here on Earth while you anticipate the amazing life waiting for you in heaven.

---

*"For I know the plans I have for you," says the LORD.
"They are plans for good and not for disaster,
to give you a future and a hope."*
JEREMIAH 29:11

WANTING WHAT GOD
HASN'T GIVEN YOU

Some ulcers are caused by inflammation of the wishbone.

Like the love of money, envy can lead to all kinds of evil. Envy begins when we see someone else who has what we want, and our desire is to have it for ourselves.

If your heart belongs to God, you shouldn't envy what belongs to someone else. Instead, you should be glad for that person. That may be difficult to do, but you can rest in the knowledge that God has the ability to give you what you desire. In fact, He wants to give you such things, but not if those things will draw you away from Him.

If there is something you desire, and if God hasn't given it to you, He has a reason. Don't be envious of anything that God doesn't want you to have.

You are jealous for what others have, and you can't possess it,
so you fight and quarrel to take it away from them.
And yet the reason you don't have what you want is
that you don't ask God for it. And even when you do ask,
you don't get it because your whole motive is wrong—
you want only what will give you pleasure.
JAMES 4:2–3

TRUST IN GOD

Faith does not demand miracles but often accomplishes them.

Whenever we believe that God is going to do something because we need it right now, we put our faith in the wrong place. "I need a miracle, God, and I need it by tomorrow," you might say. So you pray and believe God will do it, and sometimes He gives you a miracle. But what if He doesn't? Is your faith inadequate, or does God have something else to teach you?

Actually, both things could be true, and here's why. When your faith demands miracles, you are merely putting your faith in faith. You think that if you believe hard enough, God will do something. The problem isn't your belief. You just aren't believing in God. Faith takes tremendous effort, but it is much more effective when you put your complete trust in God rather than in what you need from God. That's where the miracles begin.

"I do believe, but help me not to doubt!"
MARK 9:24

PROMISES

Rest on God's promises; stand behind your own.

Aren't you glad that God keeps His promises? Wouldn't it be terrible if He were unreliable or kept changing His mind? We would always be worrying about whether God was changing His plan of salvation. Our spiritual life would be in constant turmoil and filled with uncertainty. But God isn't like that. He never changes. He keeps His promises. He is totally reliable. And because He is, we can relax in our relationship with Him.

Other people need to have the same sense of certainty in their relationships with you. They need to know that you are reliable and that you keep your promises. If you have trouble keeping your promises, then don't be so quick to make them. Promise less than you expect to do, so you can deliver more than you promised.

Reflect God's character by being true to your word.

And by that same mighty power,
he has given us all of his
rich and wonderful promises.
2 PETER 1:4

THE MOST IMPORTANT APPOINTMENT

*Make an appointment with God every day
and then keep it as if you were meeting with
the most important person in the world.*

W_e all carry appointment calendars. Some of us have day planners, and others can't go anywhere without their Palm Pilots. A few even have assistants to help them sort out their appointments and tasks. Why all the fuss? So we can stay on task and keep our appointments. We don't want to miss out on anything or anyone that would help improve our lives. Neither do we want to disappoint anybody who wants to meet with us.

That said, does it seem like a good idea to put God at the top of your appointment list? Of course it does. He's the most important person in the world to you, and His plans for you are the most important tasks. Seek God and what He wants for you every day, and to help you remember, put His name in your appointment book. That's one daily meeting you don't want to miss.

In the morning you will see the glorious presence of the LORD.
EXODUS 16:7

PRIORITIES

Priorities are like flowers; they are best when arranged properly.

Has anyone ever told you to "arrange your priorities"? They're really asking you to put the goals and events of your life in order of importance. Where should your priorities begin and end? Should they be unique to you? Should you establish short-term priorities, or should you take the more long-term view?

God has deliberately called you out of the ordinary activities of life to a higher level of living. He doesn't want you to worry about your short-term personal needs (because He will provide them). Instead, He wants you to structure your life in a way that makes Him your highest priority. When you arrange your priorities in that fashion, then everything else will fall into its proper place. Can you say that you have made God your top priority? Does your daily schedule confirm or deny it?

No, O people,
the LORD has already told you what is good,
and this is what he requires:
to do what is right, to love mercy,
and to walk humbly with your God.
MICAH 6:8

AVOIDING TEMPTATION

*You are less likely to fall into temptation if
you don't walk along the edge.*

We all struggle with temptation. When we yield to it, we usually blame it on our weakness. But it's not always a matter of weakness. Sometimes it is just a matter of plain stupidity. We stupidly put ourselves in the path of temptation when we could have avoided it altogether.

Start being smart about resisting temptation. If you know that you are having difficulty with a particular sin, then arrange the circumstances of your life so that you aren't confronted with the temptation as often. Decide ahead of time what you won't do, where you won't go, and what you won't watch. You might even have to disassociate with a few "friends" who are leading you into trouble.

The hardest time to resist temptation is when you're knee-deep in it. It's just a lot easier to stay away from it to begin with.

---

*So humble yourselves before God. Resist the Devil,
and he will flee from you.*
JAMES 4:7

USE YOUR BURDENS

Don't pray for a lighter load. Pray for a stronger back.

When you ask God to take away your burdens, you deny yourself the opportunity to grow in your faith. You don't get smarter by studying less, you don't get into better shape by becoming inactive, and you don't grow in your faith by escaping your burdens. We don't believe in God because life is easy and we have everything we need. We come to God because we recognize our desperate situation. And once we align ourselves with God personally through Christ, our faith grows because we are aware we need Christ in us to live each day.

You become a Christian by believing that God can save you through Christ. You grow as a Christian by believing that God is allowing the burdens in your life to strengthen you, and that you can overcome them in Christ.

You can be sure that the more we suffer for Christ,
the more God will shower us
with his comfort through Christ.
2 CORINTHIANS 1:5

GOALS

A goal is worthy only if it heads you in the right direction.

Studies have shown that people who set goals are more successful than people who don't. Whether it is losing weight or saving money, goals encourage people to improve.

The best goal you could ever have is to know God better. All of your energy should be focused on being like Christ in your actions and your thoughts. Of course, Christ was perfect, and you will never make it to perfection (in this lifetime). But as you move toward your goal, your life will improve. That doesn't mean that your life will be trouble-free, but everything else will seem insignificant compared to the indescribable wonder of knowing God and realizing His love for you. Now that is a goal worth pursuing. Go for it.

I am focusing all my energies on this one thing:
Forgetting the past and looking forward to what lies ahead,
I strain to reach the end of the race
and receive the prize for which God,
through Christ Jesus, is calling us up to heaven.
PHILIPPIANS 3:13–14

DISCIPLINE

Discipline is at the heart of discipleship.

Psst! It's okay to read this. We aren't talking about the "punishment" type of discipline. (We'll sneak that in under a pleasant-sounding title.) The kind of discipline that we're talking about today is a regular routine—a habit—a repeated action that produces a benefit.

Following God requires that you stay in spiritual shape. And you can stay spiritually fit only if you stay in training. Spiritual training requires a daily regime of studying God's Word and spending quality time with Him in prayer.

Exercising only once a week won't keep you physically fit. And you can't really know God by going to church only once a week. If you are serious about knowing God and following Him, you'll be serious about your spiritual fitness program.

All athletes practice strict self-control.
They do it to win a prize that will fade away,
but we do it for an eternal prize.
1 CORINTHIANS 9:25

REAL LIFE

Your life will have meaning in the physical realm
only when your life takes on meaning in the spiritual realm.

Many people are fascinated with the possibility of life in the spiritual realm. A spiritual dimension could give more meaning to earthly existence and could have implications for life after death. How does someone make a connection between the physical world and the spiritual realm?

That's what a religious leader named Nicodemus wanted to know. He asked Jesus how someone in the natural world could enter the spiritual realm. Jesus told him that real life on Earth and eternal life in heaven are possible only when a person is "born again." Religious activities are not enough to enter God's spiritual realm. It takes a spiritual rebirth that happens through a belief in and a relationship with Jesus Himself.

"Humans can reproduce only human life,
but the Holy Spirit gives new life from heaven."
JOHN 3:6

PURPOSE

A sense of purpose gives energy to your mind
and enthusiasm to your heart.

Do you ever wonder about your purpose in life? What will bring you meaning and fulfillment? That is a fairly deep philosophical question, but the answer isn't too complicated.

As a person who loves God, you know that fulfillment doesn't come from temporal endeavors. True purpose can be found only in matters that have eternal significance. You also know that a meaningful life is not self-centered, but it is outwardly directed to other people.

If you combine these two concepts, you must come to the conclusion that a part of God's purpose for your life is to tell people about Him. Only God, through Christ, can change a life for eternity, and He has called you to deliver that message. He has called you for that purpose.

"Go into all the world
and preach the Good News
to everyone, everywhere."
MARK 16:15

Turn on the Ignition

The next time you feel weak in the knees,
try using them to pray.

Prayer is a powerful tool because it activates the power of God in your life. God is always with you through the presence of the Holy Spirit, but He won't unleash His power unless you ask Him to, and the way you ask is through prayer (John 16:24). Think of your life as a car (you choose what kind of car you want to be). God is the engine that powers you, and the Holy Spirit is the fuel. But unless you turn on the ignition by praying, you're going to sit there, nice to look at, but going nowhere. Prayer is like the spark that ignites the Holy Spirit to drive God's power.

Oh, and there's one more aspect to our little illustration. You need a road map to tell you where you need to go. That would be the Bible, God's personal atlas for your life. Don't leave home without it.

So let us come boldly to the throne of our gracious God.
There we will receive his mercy,
and we will find grace to help us when we need it.
Hebrews 4:16

CHALLENGES

Learn to thrive on challenge and change.

Don't think that your life will be totally serene and tranquil if you let God lead you. Yes, He is a God of comfort, but He never promised that He would remove all of the problems and troubles from your life. If fact, He promised just the opposite. The Bible says that you can expect tough times. But God equips you to handle anything that He allows to come your way.

You shouldn't shy away from changes and challenges when you know that God is on your side. You should look forward to them. Oh, sure, you may be nervous because you don't know what's coming next. But that feeling keeps you dependent upon God (which is a very good thing).

As God allows challenges into your life, don't worry about being pushed out of your comfort zone. You aren't really being pushed out of it. God is just enlarging it.

But those who wait on the LORD will find new strength.
They will fly high on wings like eagles.
They will run and not grow weary.
They will walk and not faint.
ISAIAH 40:31

THE KEY TO KNOWING YOURSELF

If you want to know yourself better,
get to know your Creator better.

It seems like everybody is trying to get to know themselves better, and there are plenty of people ready to tell you how to "tap the power within" or get acquainted with "your inner child."

While there is value to knowing what you can do to improve your life, we would suggest that you spend more time focused on God than on yourself. Studying and learning about *you* shouldn't be that big a deal. After all, you're with yourself twenty-four hours a day. But God is different (and aren't we glad). Studying and learning about Him takes a lifetime, and even then you barely scratch the surface.

Besides, getting to know God better inevitably leads to knowing yourself better. God created you in His own image. His imprint is on your life. As you get closer to God, you will get closer to the real you.

We ask God to give you a complete understanding of
what he wants to do in your lives,
and we ask him to make you wise with spiritual wisdom.
COLOSSIANS 1:9

DEATH

Death is not the end of your life's story;
it is just the end of a chapter.

You can tell that our society is uncomfortable with the concept of *death*. No one wants to use that word, so we have developed lots of euphemisms for death and dying. We say that someone *expired*; or he *passed away*; or he *bit the big burrito*. (Okay, maybe that last one is unique to California.)

The one euphemism that is incorrect is *grand finale*. Death isn't the final curtain. God has placed within each of us an eternal soul. From the moment of our conception, that soul exists forever. Our physical death is merely the cessation of our biological being, but our soul lives on. For this reason, we should have no fear of death because it is not our end. For those who know and love God, death is the beginning of the best part of their life.

"Death is swallowed up in victory.
O death, where is your victory?
O death, where is your sting?"
1 CORINTHIANS 15:54–55

Like a Mirror

When you ask God to change you,
He will make you more like Him.

Every person is born with God's imprint (Gen. 1:27), but every person is also born with sin's imprint (Rom. 3:23). Those two imprints aren't equal, but sin obstructs our view of God and our longing for Him (think of a dark cloud blocking the sun). God is much more powerful than our sins, but He won't take them away until we ask Him to (1 John 1:9).

Then and only then can the Spirit of God begin His work in our lives, which is to completely transform us and turn us into people who represent our heavenly Father here on Earth. If it all sounds very mystical, there's a reason. It's a mystical process! But it isn't fairy tale stuff. This is completely real. As God builds His character into ours through the Holy Spirit, we become like mirrors reflecting His imprint and His glory, which others can clearly see.

As the Spirit of the Lord works within us,
we become more and more like him
and reflect his glory even more.
2 Corinthians 3:18

RESPECT

Like all moral values, respect is caught more than it is taught.

Respect for authority has deteriorated in our society. Some of the erosion is due to the blatant failing of our leaders. (Their despicable conduct makes it impossible to respect them.) But much of the disrespect for authority comes from a selfish nature that does not want to subject itself to someone else's control or leadership.

The loss of respect for authority is not limited to the social area. It is very prevalent in the spiritual realm. And you may be guilty of it yourself. Do you respect God? After all, He is the all-powerful, all-knowing, all-loving God Who is intimately involved in the universe and in your life. You flagrantly disrespect Him when you are too busy to include Him in your life. You dishonor Him when you pursue your own petty desires instead of His plan.

Everyone deserves your respect, and it will be easier to give it to them if you start by respecting God.

Show respect for everyone.
Love your Christian brothers and sisters.
Fear God. Show respect for the king.
1 PETER 2:17

ADMIT YOUR MISTAKES

*It's hard to learn from a mistake that
you don't acknowledge making.*

What are the three hardest words to say? The correct answer is "I was wrong." (We'll give you partial credit if you are a guy and answered "I am lost.") Admitting a mistake is difficult for anyone, but there are some important reasons why you should.

You are being stubborn and prideful if you aren't willing to admit your mistakes. If you refuse to deal with the reality of your mistakes, you're likely to keep making them. If you are making spiritual mistakes, then your relationship with God will be interrupted as long as you refuse to admit to God that you have done wrong.

Don't hesitate to talk to God about your mistakes. After all, He noticed when you made them. (And He even knew that you'd make them before they happened.) And He still loves you.

---

*But no, you won't listen.
So you are storing up terrible punishment for yourself
because of your stubbornness in refusing to turn from your sin.*
ROMANS 2:5

KEEP THE TRUTH TOGETHER

People of integrity make an easy target for critics because they stand upright.

Telling the truth has become a lost art. It's not that we're out there telling lies (although there is plenty of that going on). We're just not telling "the truth, the whole truth, and nothing but the truth." We sort of sneak up on the truth, circle the truth, tell part of the truth, but don't come right out and tell the whole truth. We give out just enough information to keep us out of trouble, but not enough to honor God.

When God asks us to be truthful, He isn't suggesting that we pick out the parts that make us look good. He wants us to deal in whole truth. That's what it means to have integrity: to be "whole." If you want to be a person of integrity, don't break the truth into pieces. Keep it together, even if it invites criticism.

People with integrity have firm footing,
but those who follow crooked paths will slip and fall.
PROVERBS 10:9

CRISIS

*The best way to minimize a crisis is to
compare it to your blessings.*

You want a tranquil life, but you don't always get what you want. At some unexpected time, you'll be hit by a crisis. It might be severe financial reverses, or sickness, or even death. It may be rebellious children or a fractured marriage. You may have no control over the events, but you can choose your response.

Consider that your crisis can be an opportunity to grow closer to God. Perhaps you have been ignoring Him in "the good times." (While you might never admit this, your actions might indicate otherwise.) When the money runs out, or your health is in jeopardy, or the children are in trouble, you can turn to God and He will be there. No appointment is necessary. You don't have to take a number. And you won't get stuck with His voice mail. It won't remain a crisis if God is in charge.

---

*Those who plant in tears will harvest with shouts of joy.
They weep as they go to plant their seed,
but they sing as they return with the harvest.*
PSALM 126:5–6

DECLARE YOUR DEPENDENCE

*It's good to declare your independence,
but it's even better to declare your dependence on God.*

The Declaration of Independence happened long before 1776. In fact, humankind declared its independence from God in the Garden of Eden when Adam and Eve believed the lie that they could live independent of God. Since then, we humans have been constantly struggling to do it our way.

God knows that true independence is impossible. There's no way we can function effectively if we are cut off from His help. We are like branches in a vineyard. Once cut off, we die. Jesus is the true vine (John 15:1), and unless we are connected to Him, we will never truly be productive. And our so-called independence won't lead to freedom but to our own destruction.

---

*"Remain in me, and I will remain in you.
For a branch cannot produce fruit if it is severed from the vine,
and you cannot be fruitful apart from me."*
JOHN 15:4

WORK ON YOUR CHARACTER

Character is made by what you stand for;
reputation by what you fall for.

Character and reputation are closely related, but they come about in very different ways. Your character takes a long time to develop—a lifetime, in fact. It's a work that's always in progress, and it is built in small increments. Your reputation, on the other hand, depends on how you respond in certain situations. You become known as "courageous," "tough-minded," "decisive," or "trustworthy" because of the predictable actions that come out of your character.

It's more important to work on your character than your reputation, because your reputation can change if you make wrong decisions or encounter some obstacles that cause you to falter. When this happens, don't worry. Your reputation will return—stronger than ever—as long as your character is rooted in God and not in your own strength.

"Unless you are faithful in small matters,
you won't be faithful in large ones.
If you cheat even a little,
you won't be honest with greater responsibilities."
LUKE 16:10

DESTINATION

Focus on where you are going rather than where you are now.

L et's admit it. Life on this earth can get pretty lousy sometimes if you are sincerely trying to follow God. There are a lot of people who are very hostile toward anyone who tries to bring a godly influence into society. If they identify you as "one of those," then you're a target for criticism and sarcasm. Get ready to be yelled at, berated, and belittled.

When you've been emotionally abused for your faith, just remember that this life is not your final destination. It's only transitory. There is a whole new life—without end— waiting ahead for you. You can look forward to time everlasting with God Himself. The best is yet to come. (And it will last a lot longer than your short stay here on Earth. In fact, it will seem like an eternity—because it will be.)

*"God blesses you when you are
mocked and persecuted and lied about
because you are my followers.
Be happy about it! Be very glad!
For a great reward awaits you in heaven."*
MATTHEW 5:11–12

CAUSE AND EFFECT

The naïve person underestimates God;
the foolish person ignores Him.

Did you ever do something wrong but didn't care because the consequences seemed insignificant? Everything we say and do has a consequence, no matter how small. Maybe you can fool other people, but you can't fool God. He knows what you do, and He says that there are eternal consequences to your actions. If you do whatever you want for your own purposes without regard to God, then the consequences of your behavior will lead to your eternal spiritual death and destruction (that sounds pretty harsh, but that's what the Bible says).

On the other hand, if you try to live a life that pleases God, then the consequences of your actions "will reap a harvest of blessing at the appropriate time" (Gal. 6:9).

You will always reap what you sow!
Those who live only to satisfy their own sinful desires
will harvest the consequences of decay and death.
But those who live to please the Spirit
will harvest everlasting life from the Spirit.
GALATIANS 6:7–8

AMBITION

*Since God knows what is best for you,
make sure your ambitions are aligned with His directions.*

Ambition is natural. After all, you want a happy family, friendships, financial security, and good health. In other words, you want a great life. It's only natural to have such ambitions and to do everything necessary to attain your goals. But should you be ambitious just because it comes naturally?

Jesus taught about the great irony of self-ambition. He said you must lose your life in order to keep it. This paradox forces you to choose which is more important: your physical life or your eternal soul. Jesus taught that gaining everything on Earth—all the things that are supposed to make you happy—will still leave you emotionally bankrupt if you don't have a spiritual relationship with God.

God wants you to live with ambition and purpose, but He doesn't want your focus to be self-centered. Let God be your priority. Let living for His Kingdom be your ambition.

*"And how do you benefit if you gain the whole world
but lose or forfeit your own soul in the process?"*
LUKE 9:25

HAVE PATIENCE

True patience comes when you wait on God's timing
rather than your own.

There are some character qualities you can have without experiencing any downside. For example, you don't have to resist the temptation to lie in order to have integrity. That character trait can stand all by itself. On the other hand, there are character qualities that don't exist without a downside. Patience is one of those.

It's impossible to have patience unless you first have to wait. It's the waiting, which for most of us is difficult and unpleasant, which brings about the virtue of patience. You shouldn't be looking for opportunities to lie just so you can resist and claim integrity as part of your character, but it's an honorable thing to look for ways to wait so you can develop your patience. And what is the highest form of patience? Waiting on the Lord. That's where your patience is at its highest point.

But if we look forward to something we don't have yet,
we must wait patiently and confidently.
ROMANS 8:25

THE BEAUTY OF HONESTY

*Being honest saves you time because
you don't have to spend extra hours covering your tracks.*

Honesty is like the glue that holds relationships together. Whether you are dealing with a spouse, a friend, or a business partner, honesty brings trust and loyalty to the relationship. On the other hand, dishonesty and deceit can tear the relationship apart. A lie will lead to embarrassment, anger, and a loss of trust that cannot be easily rebuilt.

Don't get caught in the trap of devising excuses for dishonesty. There are no loopholes, and there is no such thing as a "white lie." When you are tempted to violate the truth, ignore the excuses and look at your motives. Why would you want to jeopardize the relationship with the virus of dishonesty? Is it to protect you?

Although the truth does not always come easily, God will honor you if you live honestly before Him.

It is an honor to receive an honest reply.
PROVERBS 24:26

Baby Talk

God is looking for coordinated Christians
whose walk matches their talk.

Have you ever watched a baby in the early stages of walking? The little guy steps cautiously, then wobbles as he gets his balance, takes some faltering steps, finally falling on his well-padded bottom. Everybody laughs, including the baby, who is jabbering nonsense while drooling uncontrollably.

It's funny in a baby, but rather sad in a full-grown adult. Yet that's the way some Christians live out their spiritual lives. They walk like babies, jabber like babies, and fall on their rears like babies. Instead of growing up into full-size spiritual adults, they remain babies.

Every one of us starts out as a baby in the Lord, but God doesn't want any of us to stay that way. His desire is that we grow into spiritually mature believers whose walk and talk glorify Him.

You have been Christians a long time now,
and you ought to be teaching others.
Instead, you need someone to teach you again the basic things. . . .
You are like babies who drink only milk
and cannot eat solid food.
HEBREWS 5:12

DON'T BE A BABY

A baby being a baby is cute. An adult being a baby is annoying.

A baby grows up to be an adult automatically. There's no such thing as a baby staying a baby (at least not in the physical sense). Spiritually speaking, it's possible to stay in the baby stage for years. There are Christians who have no more spiritual maturity and discernment now than the day they were born again in Christ. How does this happen?

The main reason is that they never get beyond baby food. A new Christian can only handle spiritual "milk," which is necessary to "grow into the fullness of your salvation" (1 Pet. 2:2). Milk includes the basics of your faith. It's spiritual kindergarten, and we all have to go through it.

Eventually we need to move beyond the basics to the deeper truths of God. This takes consistent study, prayer, and fellowship with other mature believers. In other words, it takes effort. Without it, we remain babies.

And a person who is living on milk
isn't very far along in the Christian life
and doesn't know much about doing what is right.
HEBREWS 5:13

What You Have to Give

An inheritance can improve the conveniences of life,
but a heritage can improve the character of life.

There is an art to gift giving. To select the perfect gift, you have to know what the recipient needs. You'll also want to choose a gift that will be appreciated and have some long-lasting value. These guidelines are useful for the usual gift-giving occasions, but they are also relevant in a spiritual context.

There is a gift of a spiritual nature that you can give to your family and friends. It is a consistent testimony of a life committed wholeheartedly to God. This is a gift they need, because your example may draw them closer to God.

For you have heard my vows, O God.
You have given me an inheritance reserved for
those who fear your name.
PSALM 61:5

LEARN FROM A PET?

Caring for your pet means more than feeding.

Our pets can teach us a lot. The most obvious lesson we can learn is responsibility. You have to feed the dog, clean up after the dog, and exercise the dog. Our pets are totally dependent upon us for their welfare and well-being.

It isn't that much of a stretch to compare the way we provide for our pets to the way God provides for us. That doesn't mean that we are God's little pets. He didn't create us for His amusement. He doesn't expect us to roll over so He can scratch our bellies. In fact, God created us in His image, so there is a likeness between God and us.

The comparison with pets has more to do with care and feeding. Just as our pets are totally dependent on us for their existence, we are completely dependent on God for all that we are and all that we have.

The godly are concerned for the welfare of their animals.
PROVERBS 12:10

NOTORIETY

Strive to be a person of faith rather than fame.

Admit it. You like to be popular and well liked. We all do. Oh, sure, you don't want to go overboard with it (you'd like to keep your picture off the cover of the *National Enquirer*), but you certainly don't want to be ostracized from any group.

Your desire to be well liked can be at odds with your faith in God. Claiming the name of Christ may alienate you from some groups. Jesus isn't very "politically correct" in most of society. It is okay to have "faith" in Mother Nature, or a belief in some nondescript universal power, but you're setting yourself up to be scoffed at and shunned if you proclaim a belief in the God of the Bible.

Don't let your desire to be well liked impede your faith. The popularity of your friends is fickle, but God's love for you is forever.

"And how do you benefit if you gain the whole world
but lose your own soul in the process?
Is anything worth more than your soul?"
MATTHEW 16:26

FULLY EQUIPPED

*It's no big deal to do something on your own.
But doing something with God's help—
now there's an accomplishment.*

There's nothing we can do to earn our salvation (Eph. 2:8). The only work is the work of Christ on our behalf, and that's already been done. Once we accept God's gift of salvation, our work begins in order to accomplish the "good things" God wants us to do (Eph. 2:10).

Don't worry. God doesn't leave you on your own. He doesn't pull back once He's saved you so you can do it by yourself. God has given us His Word so we can grow into mature adult believers. As we read and study the Bible for ourselves, God will teach us through the Holy Spirit. As we sit under the teaching of mature Christians, He will show us what to do. If we make the effort to grow, God will fully equip us.

*It is God's way of preparing us in every way,
fully equipped for every good thing God wants us to do.*
2 TIMOTHY 3:17

STEWARDSHIP

Your attitude about giving reflects your attitude about God.

If you think God needs your money, you are wrong. He doesn't! After all, He owns the universe and all that is in it. So, technically, He already owns all of your money.

Although God is not dependent upon you for financial support, He is interested in how you spend your money. In fact, He wants you to use it to help others. He wants you to be generous, helping people in need and helping support the ministry of your church. Giving your money should not be done out of obligation or guilt. God wants your financial giving to be a natural expression of your love for Him and for others.

If you are really eager to give,
it isn't important how much you are able to give.
God wants you to give what you have,
not what you don't have.
2 CORINTHIANS 8:12

It's Not Enough to Believe

It's more important to believe God than to believe in God.

It's one thing to *believe in* God and quite another to *believe* God. Believing in God is no big deal. Everyone believes there is a God, because God has put that knowledge in every person's heart (Rom. 1:19). What everybody doesn't believe is God's plan to bring us back to Himself through Jesus Christ (Eph. 1:5).

How often have you heard someone say, "Oh, there are many ways to God. All that matters is that you believe." Do you believe that? Then all you are doing is believing in God, and your belief won't count for anything. On the other hand, when you believe that Jesus is God's only plan for your salvation, your belief will count for eternity (Rom. 10:9–10).

Do you *believe in* God? Great. You're a member of the human race. Do you *believe* God? Then you're a member of the family of God.

Do you still think it's enough
just to believe that there is one God?
Well, even the demons believe this, and they tremble in terror!
JAMES 2:19

REBELLION

Rebellion is usually a war of wills.

You probably don't consider yourself to be a rebellious person. Your opinion of a rebel may include a tattoo, a biker's jacket, and a defiant attitude. Well, your opinion is wrong, except for the part about the attitude. The fact that your skin is tattoo-free and your closet doesn't contain a leather jacket embroidered with a skull and crossbones doesn't mean that you aren't a rebel. It depends entirely on your mind-set.

God designed you to be an individual with your own personality and style, but your actions and attitudes need to be within His plan for your life. When you intentionally leave God out of the details of your life, you are being defiant and rebelling against His authority.

"Yet I want your will, not mine."
MATTHEW 26:39

Your Circumstances and God

*Even when you don't feel in control of your circumstances,
you can be sure that God is.*

The story of Joseph is one of the most familiar stories in the Bible. The youngest of twelve brothers, Joseph started out as the favorite son in Israel and ended up a slave in Egypt. On the surface Joseph's life was one of circumstances beyond his control. His father favored him, his brothers hated him, Pharaoh promoted him, and Pharaoh's wife lied about him.

In the end, however, God restored Joseph so he could rescue his family while preserving a nation. While it seemed that Joseph wasn't in control of his destiny, there was no question that God was with him every step of the way, directing his ways, even when the days were dark.

When it seems like circumstances are outside your control and the world is against you, remain faithful to God, especially when the days are dark. God promises to restore you for your own good and His glory.

*"As far as I am concerned,
God turned into good what you meant for evil."*
GENESIS 50:20

BE PASSIONATE ABOUT IT

It is easier to pick up your cross than to drag it along.

Life without passion isn't living; it's just existing. But living with passion doesn't happen automatically. You have to find your passion, define it, and then live it.

After you discover what you are passionate about, you'll still have to do other things. The trick is to maintain your focus. Look at Jesus. He knew exactly why He was sent to Earth—to bring God's Kingdom to the hearts of mankind—and it was His passion. While He was involved in many activities (from healing the sick to dealing with the religious authorities), He didn't allow other events in His life to distract Him or to dilute His message.

God has created you, knows your innermost thoughts, and has created a purpose for your life. Ask Him to reveal it to you, and then pursue it passionately.

But [Jesus] replied,
"I must preach the Good News of the Kingdom of God
in other places, too, because that is why I was sent."
LUKE 4:43

GET IN THE GAME

Don't run with the ball unless you know the direction of the goal.

Imagine if each of the players in a baseball game played according to their own rules. You would have total chaos. The pitcher might decide that the strike zone goes from the forehead to the ankles. The batter may decide that it takes twenty-two strikes to make an out. A base runner may decide to dispense with third base because it is more efficient to run from second base to home plate.

You can't change the rules for following God, either. You don't get to decide what "feels" right to you; God isn't going to change His divine plan to accommodate your whims. God already has a rule book, and He is anxious for you to learn His game plan.

Don't sit on the sidelines waiting to play. Get into the game.

Remember that in a race everyone runs,
but only one person gets the prize.
You also must run in such a way that you will win.
1 CORINTHIANS 9:24

THE GOOD, THE BAD, AND THE . . .

*Knowing that God knows
everything about us is very comforting.
It's also very unsettling.*

We can take comfort in the knowledge that God is intimately involved in the details of our lives. If He watches over the lowly sparrow, He watches over us and directs our way.

At the same time, because He is God, He is aware of every detail, including the stuff we'd just as soon hide from Him. God isn't directing us to engage in behavior that contradicts what He wants for us (we do that quite well on our own), but He knows everything—the bad as well as the good.

How do you feel about God knowing you completely? If you're like us, it probably gives you a certain amount of fear. That's okay, as long as our fear motivates us to take Him and His commands seriously.

---

*"He reveals deep and mysterious things
and knows what lies hidden in darkness,
though he himself is surrounded by light."*
DANIEL 2:22

TYRANNY OF THE STUFF

The fewer your desires, the richer you'll be.

There is a subtle tyranny that we live under. In theological terms it might be referred to "self" or "life," but in our vernacular it is "stuff." We have stuff, we accumulate stuff, and it seems that we always want more stuff. Our self-image is often defined by the stuff we have.

God doesn't mind your having stuff. He doesn't require that you be an absolute pauper with only so few possessions as would fit in a backpack. But God does want you to live free from the tyranny of your stuff. You shouldn't be so enamored with the stuff you have (and the new stuff you want) that it interferes with your pursuit of God. In other words, your possession of stuff is a problem only if you are afraid to give it all up if God asks you to do so. How important is your stuff to you?

Not that I was ever in need,
for I have learned how to get along happily
whether I have much or little.
PHILIPPIANS 4:11

EXPECT TO SUFFER

It's better to suffer for Christ than to live without Him.

Some people treat God like some kind of insurance policy. They're not really convinced that they need Him, except when times get tough. That's when they pull out their insurance policy and read the fine print, hoping they're covered. In other words, they expect God to protect them from any hardship.

Why should any of us expect to get through this life without suffering? If God did not spare His own Son from suffering to the point of death, who are we to think that we are exempt?

The apostle Paul knew a lot about suffering, and he wrote about it in detail. He was beaten, imprisoned, shipwrecked, jailed, and ostracized (for a complete description, read 2 Cor. 6:5–10). But he never lost hope, because he knew it was better to suffer for Christ than to live without Him.

---

*In everything we do we try to show that
we are true ministers of God.
We patiently endure troubles and hardships
and calamities of every kind.*
2 CORINTHIANS 6:4

FOLLOW YOUR LEADERS

It is easier to follow your leader if you have
confidence in whom your leader is following.

Dogs are taught to obey their masters. Children are supposed to obey their parents. But when it comes to adults, the principle of submission to authority seems to be replaced with the theory of "What's in it for me?" Before we obey—or even follow—a leader, we want that leader to prove that we are going to get some personal benefit from it.

In God's paradigm, we are supposed to willingly follow our leaders. This is particularly true in spiritual matters at your church. Your church leaders (whether you call them pastors, elders, board members, or priests) are accountable to God for your spiritual welfare. Help them do their job by following their leadership. When you obey them joyfully, you make their job easier and bring honor to God in the process.

Obey your spiritual leaders and do what they say.
Their work is to watch over your souls,
and they know they are accountable to God.
Give them reason to do this joyfully and not with sorrow.
That would certainly not be for your benefit.
HEBREWS 13:17

DON'T LET YOUR POSSESSIONS DEFINE YOU

What you have should not determine who you are.

Let's make sure that we have several things straight. First, material possessions are not a measurement of how much God loves you. (If that were the case, then Jesus—with only a tunic or two—wasn't very popular with His heavenly Father.) Secondly, material possessions aren't related to whether you are a good or a bad person. Thirdly, your possessions can become a barrier between you and God *if you let them.*

All of us spend too much time thinking about our possessions (or lack of them). Realize that your possessions are irrelevant to God (and they should be to you, too). Don't let them interfere with God's plan for your spiritual growth. Try to stay focused on God more than on your goods.

Jesus looked around and said to his disciples,
"How hard it is for rich people
to get into the Kingdom of God!"
MARK 10:23

PEACE

If you're looking for peace,
you might start by consulting the "Prince of Peace."

To the world, the concept of *peace* means the absence of war. It means living in harmony with others and enjoying public order. Those are acceptable definitions from a purely secular perspective, but they don't get to the heart of the matter from a spiritual perspective.

The peace that God offers you is freedom from *inner* conflict. It doesn't necessarily remove external discord from your circumstances, but it can replace worry and fear. When you have God's peace in your life, you are able to withstand the external discord in your life. You can relax in the assurance that someone greater than you (God) is in control of the situation. So, when you think about it, God's inner peace also affects your perspective of the external problems.

"I am leaving you with a gift—
peace of mind and heart.
And the peace I give isn't like the peace the world gives.
So don't be troubled or afraid."
JOHN 14:27

EACH NEW DAY

*The way you deal with life each day depends on
what you bring to life each day.*

How do you respond when someone asks, "How's it going with you?" If you're like most people, you reply with a bland "Same old thing." (Or, maybe you are just quirky enough to give a "Same old, same old" response.) With such an apathetic approach to life, it is no wonder that we get tired of the routine and monotony of daily existence.

Infuse your life with a little enthusiasm. Focus on the blessings that God has waiting for you each and every day. His love for you never grows stale. He does not become impatient with your spiritual immaturity. His forgiveness continues to be limitless.

Instead of being depressed by the repetitiveness of your routine, be excited by the consistency of God's love.

---

*Great is his faithfulness;
his mercies begin afresh each day.*
LAMENTATIONS 3:23

GOD'S BOOK

If you're wondering how God speaks,
commands, and leads—read the Bible.

One of the most amazing aspects of our relationship with God is that He has given each of us a personal message, and it's one we can read anytime we want. We're talking about the Bible, of course, the greatest book ever written because it is a book written by God.

Sometimes the Bible is called the Good Book. That's okay, but you need to know that the Bible is much more than a book, and it is much more than good. Here's the deal. The Bible contains the very words of God. He literally "breathed in" His words (that's what *inspired* means) into the prophets, who then wrote them down for us (2 Pet. 1:20–21). You don't have to *wonder* about God. You can *know* about God because He has left you a message. When you read the Bible, it's as if God is talking to you.

All Scripture is inspired by God.
2 TIMOTHY 3:16

READ THE INSTRUCTIONS

The Bible is the greatest instructional book in the world.

The quickest way to get things right is to read the instructions. Say you're putting together a swing set. You could try to assemble the pieces by looking at the box (most men do this first), but you'll never get it right—not until you read the instruction manual.

If you need instructions for a swing set, you certainly need instructions for life (there's not even a box to look at). None of us is capable of knowing God and understanding His plans for our lives unless we read His personal instructional book. Don't be misled by your uninformed friends. The Bible isn't a book of do's and don'ts. It is a book of how to do it right. There are a lot of opinions floating around, but you can trust the Bible as the standard for testing everything else that claims to be true.

Scripture. . .is useful to teach us what is true.
2 TIMOTHY 3:16

THE TRUTH DETECTOR

It's better to tell the truth than to avoid telling a lie.

Have you ever wondered what it would be like to take a lie detector test? When you think about it, you envision yourself in a chair with some wires taped to your forehead and your chest (or wherever it is they stick those wires), and some expert in a white shirt asking you some direct questions to see if you're telling the truth. Even if you want to tell the truth, you can see yourself sweating under the hot lights.

Don't think of the Bible as a lie detector and God as the guy asking you questions in order to trip you up. The Bible is a truth detector that shows us the right way to live. When we study God's Word and discover for ourselves how He wants us to think and act, we can easily see that anything contrary to God's standard isn't the truth at all.

Scripture [will]. . .
make us realize what is wrong in our lives.
2 TIMOTHY 3:16

STAY ON COURSE

*Having a goal means you know where you're going.
It also means you stay on course.*

The reason rocket science is so difficult is that it has to be so exact. If you are shooting for the moon and you are off by only a fraction of a degree, you will miss the target by thousands of miles. In a more down-to-earth example, if you are hanging wallpaper without a plumb line to keep you straight, you'll be way off by the time you finish the room.

All of us need something objective and outside of ourselves and our subjective thinking in order to keep us straight and true. That's why God gave us the Bible. His Word is our plumb line. The Bible is also our compass. There's not much good to staying on course if you don't know where you're going. From the Ten Commandments in the Old Testament to "love your neighbor as yourself" (Rom. 13:9) in the New Testament, the Bible gives practical advice for life.

It straightens us out and teaches us to do what is right.
2 TIMOTHY 3:16

In God's Design

Believing in fortune cookies leads to a crummy life.

Knowing God's will for your life isn't like going to a fortune-teller. It isn't a peek into the future to uncover the inevitable events that are going to happen. God's will is a relationship—you and God—that guides your behavior and your decisions.

Being in God's will doesn't give you a premonition of future events, but it does equip you with the confidence to face whatever circumstances arise. You have the assurance of believing that the One who knows you best and loves you most is directing your life. It means that both the good and bad circumstances can be used as part of God's design to bring you closer to Him.

Don't worry about trying to predict what will happen in the future. Instead, develop your relationship with God so that you can live in His will. That is your best preparation for the future.

How do you know what will happen tomorrow?
For your life is like the morning fog—
it's here a little while, then it's gone.
JAMES 4:14

SLOW THE PACE

Beware the barrenness of a busy life.

The Christian life is about relationships, not accomplishments. If you need proof of this fact, just consider that believers are referred to as *brothers and sisters* in Christ, and that we are called part of God's *family*. Although we enjoy the friendship of others, most of us don't have the time to develop meaningful relationships outside of our immediate family members. (Sometimes we don't even have time for them.) We are busy scurrying back and forth to work, helping out with the committees, and doing the errands—in other words, we are occupied with accomplishments.

God is love. If you want to reflect God in your life, then you, too, will need to show love. Love must be displayed in the context of relationships with other people. (Loving your job, or sports, or shopping doesn't count.) Carve some time out of your busy schedule to develop some meaningful friendships.

Stop loving this evil world and all that it offers you,
for when you love the world,
you show that you do not have the love of the Father in you.
1 JOHN 2:15

FINISH WHAT YOU START

*People will be more impressed by what you finish
than by what you start.*

How we love to start stuff! We begin a project with energy as we envision the wonderful result. We enter into a new relationship with enthusiasm as we anticipate the rewarding experience. But sometimes the project bogs down or the relationship sours, and rather than taking things to their proper conclusion, we quit. (Of course, we don't use the word "quit." We prefer to say we "lost interest.")

Jesus once told a parable about what it means to start something. Whatever it is, we need to see it through, or else we shouldn't start in the first place. The principle applies to material things and relationships, especially our relationship with God. Jesus was real blunt about this. God isn't something to sample and then discard when we lose interest. We are to take Him seriously and believe that when we begin our relationship with Him, we need to see it through.

"Don't begin until you count the cost."
LUKE 14:28

God Will See It Through

God always finishes what He starts.

Here's something we can be sure of. Once God starts a relationship with us, He's going to finish it. God paid such a high price by sending His only Son to die for our sins that He's not about to lose what rightfully belongs to Him. That's exactly what happens when we accept God's provision for our salvation—we belong to Christ like sheep belong to a shepherd. Jesus, the Great Shepherd, said this about His sheep: "I give them eternal life, and they will never perish. No one will snatch them away from me, for my Father has given them to me, and he is more powerful than anyone else. So no one can take them from me" (John 10:28–29).

Let the words of Christ give you hope today and the assurance you need tomorrow that God is going to finish what He started.

We do this by keeping our eyes on Jesus,
on whom our faith depends from start to finish.
HEBREWS 12:2

A BALANCED LIFE

Live somewhere between complacency and crisis.

Let's think for a moment about *complacency*. It has both good and bad connotations. On the good side, it conveys a sense of being satisfied with *what you have*. (And that is how you should be.) But complacency also suggests that you are satisfied in staying *where you are*—not *where* in geographic terms, but in a growth and development sense.

Many people are afraid to grow spiritually because they don't want to be stretched. They suspect that the process will involve some awkwardness or discomfort. They don't want to do anything that might make them uncomfortable. (In other words, they are complacent.)

Don't be afraid to let God move you along. Don't settle for spiritual stagnation. He is fully able to uphold you in the process of spiritual growth.

God is our refuge and strength,
always ready to help in times of trouble.
PSALM 46:1

ANXIETY ADDICTION

Anxiety is short-lived if we give it to God.

What comes to mind when you think of addiction? Alcohol. Drugs. Chocolate. How about this one: anxiety. Does it surprise you that we would consider anxiety to be an addiction? Well, it must be. Why else would people hold on to their worries when they don't have to?

Anxiety is an unproductive activity. It doesn't accomplish anything positive (although it has plenty of negative effects, such as stress, high blood pressure, and ulcers). You would think that people would try to get rid of their worries if it were possible to do so. And it is! Let God be responsible for the situation.

It won't take you twelve steps to get over your anxiety addiction. It just takes one: Give your worries to God.

The LORD is good.
When trouble comes, he is a strong refuge.
And he knows everyone who trusts in him.
NAHUM 1:7

GOD IS RELENTLESS

You might as well face God,
because it's impossible to get away from Him.

God is loving, God is forgiving, and God is gracious. That's why we can go to Him at any time for anything. King David wrote: "For the LORD is good. His unfailing love continues forever, and his faithfulness continues to each generation" (Ps. 100:5).

But along with His goodness and grace, we have to remember that God is also holy and just. He is pleased with those who give their hearts to Him, but He does not accept the rebellion of those who remain His enemies. The biggest mistake anyone can make is to think they can oppose God and get away with it. You can't fight God and win. You can't shake your fist at God and get away with it. Another mistake is to believe that God doesn't pursue us. Of course He does. God pursues us until we turn to Him, and if we don't, He keeps on coming.

The LORD is good. . . .
But he sweeps away his enemies in an overwhelming flood.
He pursues his foes into the darkness of night.
NAHUM 1:7–8

ADVERSITY

*God will either protect you from hardships
or give you the strength to go through them.
Either way, you're covered.*

People with a naïve view of God often think that He will insulate their life from hardships. If that were true, then everyone in the world would turn to God. But He doesn't choose to be everyone's good luck charm. He wants their love without any form of bribery. So, as long as we live in this world, God doesn't exempt us from the natural consequences of life. This means that you don't have a "Get Out of Jail Free" that allows you to skip calamities and misfortune.

But God hasn't left you stranded and helpless. He has given you the Holy Spirit to be His special presence *in your life*. Consequently, you have all of the spiritual and emotional strength you will need to handle the adversities that life brings your way.

---

*"I have told you all this so that you may have peace in me.
Here on earth you will have many trials and sorrows.
But take heart, because I have overcome the world."*
JOHN 16:33

SURVIVING CRITICISM

*A thick skin and a short memory are
the best weapons against unjust criticism.*

Few things hurt worse than criticism. A broken bone is painful, but it happens accidentally, and after a while the injury has healed and is forgotten. Criticism, however, is always intentionally inflicted. It is a personal attack. It often leaves a wound of bitterness and resentment. You don't easily forget criticism. (You are reminded of it whenever you see the person who said it.)

God is the only person to Whom you can go without worry that you will be criticized. He is the shelter that protects you. While He may not always be pleased with the choices that you make, His love for you is unconditional.

It is easier to accept criticism when you know that God accepts you.

---

*You hide them in the shelter of your presence,
safe from those who conspire against them.
You shelter them in your presence,
far from accusing tongues.*
PSALM 31:20

DEALING WITH DIFFICULTIES

It is possible for God to give you comfort
without removing any of your difficulties.

The easiest way to handle difficulties in your life is to change your perspective about them. Let's face it. You are going to have problems. (We aren't telling you anything that you don't already know.) But you don't have to look at them that way.

Realize that you will know God better only as your faith grows, and trusting Him in the midst of difficulties is one way to achieve that result. If God wanted to remove all of the problems from your life, He could. But don't count on it. He allows you to go through struggles so you can experience His comfort, His faithfulness, and His presence.

It seems strange to say that you can find joy in the middle of your difficulties, but you can—because it is in problems that your faith brings you closer to God.

Dear brothers and sisters, whenever trouble comes your way,
let it be an opportunity for joy.
For when your faith is tested,
your endurance has a chance to grow.
JAMES 1:2–3

FACING WHAT'S AHEAD

You can't enjoy the present if you fear the future.

Part of the fun of a vacation is the anticipation. For months in advance you can be excited about what will happen in the future. But your future isn't all filled with vacations. There are uncertainties ahead of you, and they aren't as much fun to anticipate.

Don't dwell on what you don't know about the future. It won't do you any good to worry about it. (And you're probably imagining that things will be worse than will actually be the case.) Whether your concerns for the future are about finances, or relationships, or health, trust that God will be there with you when the future happens.

In the meantime, enjoy the present.

"So don't worry about tomorrow,
for tomorrow will bring its own worries."
MATTHEW 6:34

What Is Your Motive?

The more important the task,
the more you need to examine your motives.

Why do you do what you do? Is it to please others and win their approval, or do you live to please God? How do you please God? By telling others about the Good News of Jesus.

Even when you tell others about Jesus, you need to examine your motives. How are you approaching people? If you try to convince them by complimenting them or by trying to adapt the Good News to their lifestyle, you're not presenting God's message honestly. You shouldn't live for the praise and approval of others, especially when you witness.

Jesus never compromised His message by being anything other than a servant. You should do the same. Besides, you can't fool God. He knows the motives of every heart.

Never once did we try to win you with flattery,
as you very well know.
1 Thessalonians 2:5

ULTIMATE COMFORT

Your ultimate comfort is knowing that God is with you.

When small children fall and hurt themselves, they instinctively know what to do. They turn and run to a parent. Once embraced in loving arms, the crying can subside and the pain is relieved. As an adult, you probably don't fall down very much (unless you're extremely uncoordinated). But there are plenty of occasions in life when the going is very tough, and you get bumped and bruised by the circumstances of life.

You are never too old to turn to your heavenly Father for comfort. Think of Him as standing behind you with His arms outstretched to embrace you. After your "fall," turn to Him immediately. He won't be occupied with something else. He'll pick you up and comfort you.

We who have fled to [God] for refuge can take new courage,
for we can hold on to his promise with confidence.
HEBREWS 6:18

COMPLIMENTS

Thoughtful compliments wear better than impulsive flattery.

You are wary of insincere friendships, and we don't blame you. So many people bring ulterior motives into a friendship. It is hard to know whether they are really interested in you as a friend, or whether they just want to get something from you or sell something to you. Skepticism is natural if the dinner party turns into a pitch for membership in a Yugoslavian time-share resort.

You can pave the way for meaningful friendships if you dispense with flattery. It is always shallow and usually transparent. It creates an atmosphere of insincerity in the relationship.

Make your conversation count. Learn to give compliments that are meaningful and appropriate. A legitimate, sincere compliment shows that you are aware and appreciative of someone else's effort. That is the stuff on which real friendships are built.

And God is our witness that we were not just pretending
to be your friends so you would give us money!
1 THESSALONIANS 2:5

CHEERFULNESS

A pleasant expression increases your face value.

If society has a poor impression of Christians, it is no one's fault but our own. We aren't always a happy bunch. We spend too much time being critical, and far too little time being cheerful. Many of us walk around with an expression that looks like we have been sucking on a sour pickle.

When you think about it, the people who are in love with God should be the happiest people on Earth. We have God on our side to help us through each day, and we know that our future includes an eternity with Him in heaven.

You have the knowledge of God in your mind, and you have the love of God in your heart. Make sure your face knows about it.

A cheerful heart is good medicine,
but a broken spirit saps a person's strength.
PROVERBS 17:22

SILENCE IS GOLDEN

Make moments of stillness, quiet,
and solitude part of your daily routine.

If there's one thing we need in the midst of our busy, loud, and nervous lives, it's the inner peace and quiet and assurance that only God can give. It's the only way to see God's purpose for us.

The thing is, God doesn't yell out and say, "Hey, you're neglecting me. Sit still for a moment so you can hear me." Oh, He is fully capable of getting your attention, but you don't want to make a habit of giving God a reason to chase you down (and He will).

Rather than waiting for God to whack you over the head, wouldn't it be far better to give God some time each day to quietly speak to you? But be forewarned. Being quiet before God may be one of the hardest things you will ever do. But it may also be the most important.

I am silent before you; I won't say a word.
PSALM 39:9

THANKFULNESS

Never expect gratitude, but always express appreciation.

You'll be constantly disappointed if you are expecting gratitude from people for whatever you do. Your hard work is most likely appreciated, but few people will have the sensitivity to say anything to you about it. Most people won't even stop to consider that anyone is responsible. They'll just enjoy the benefits of your labor without any expression of thankfulness.

You can learn a valuable lesson from the people who never convey their gratitude: Don't be like that. Express your appreciation when someone does something for you. It may be an employee, or a waiter, or a family member. Throughout your entire day, people are engaged in activities that help you in some way. Develop the habit of expressing your gratitude to them. (And while you're at it, remember to thank God for all that He continues to do for you.)

It is good to give thanks to the LORD,
to sing praises to the Most High.
It is good to proclaim your unfailing love in the morning,
your faithfulness in the evening.
PSALM 92:1–2

THE TRUTH ABOUT STORIES

Learn to tell a good story.

Great storytellers are great communicators. Jesus Christ, the greatest communicator of all, used stories throughout His ministry on Earth (the Bible word for His stories is *parables*). Just about half of His words as recorded in the four Gospels are in the form of stories.

You can learn to tell a good story and use illustrations and anecdotes in your speech. But it takes lots of listening and reading and practice. Why should you do it? Because good stories help you communicate and clarify the truth. One of your responsibilities as a Christian is to "correctly explain the word of truth" (2 Tim. 2:15). You can use logic and reasoning to explain the truth, but people aren't always willing to listen to your ideas. However, they will always listen to your stories, especially if they are from your own life.

Here is another story Jesus told. . .
MATTHEW 13:24

SAYING AND DOING

Being a good example is better than giving good advice.

Kids have little respect for a parent who says, "Do what I say, not what I do." Employees aren't likely to admire a boss who says the same thing. Bosses think that the hypocrisy of what they have been *doing* has gone unnoticed by the employees; parents know that any inconsistent action on their part will be noticed, and remembered, by their children.

Any point that you try to make with words will be disregarded if your actions suggest that you don't believe what you are saying. This principle is particularly true when you talk to other people about God. You won't be an effective representative for Him if you talk one way and live another. You take God's reputation with you wherever you go. Make sure that your conduct is consistent with what you have been saying about Him. People are watching more than they are listening.

And whatever you do or say,
let it be as a representative of the Lord Jesus,
all the while giving thanks through him to God the Father.
COLOSSIANS 3:17

KEEP READING

Leaders are readers.

Everyone wants to follow a leader who is informed and wise, but nobody wants to follow a leader who is a know-it-all. There is a substantial distinction between the two types. Wise leaders know that they can learn from others. The know-it-alls think that there is nothing that others can add to their vast storehouse of knowledge.

Effective leaders are anxious to gain insights from other sources. This usually means reading books and articles on the subjects that are relevant to their responsibilities. The Bible is the best book for this purpose. It deals with the dynamics of personal relationships, and that is what leadership is all about.

If you are in a position of responsibility, make the Bible your leadership manual.

Study this Book of the Law continually.
Meditate on it day and night so you may be sure
to obey all that is written in it.
Only then will you succeed.
JOSHUA 1:8

THE GREATEST AUTHOR IN THE WORLD

*Next time you read a really good book,
make every effort to get in touch with the author.*

Have you ever corresponded with an author? (If you haven't, we'd love to be your first. Our address is in the back of this book.) It can be a very rewarding experience, especially if the author responds to you.

We once met one of our favorite authors in person. He didn't know who we were, but that didn't matter. It was a thrill just to meet him. We're sure it did more for us than for him.

As exciting as it is to meet an author, the greatest privilege we have is to get in touch with the greatest Author in the world. That's right. God is an author, and His book is the world's best-seller. Go ahead. Tell God how much you enjoy His book. We guarantee He will know who you are, and He'll enjoy the experience just as much as you do.

*And being made perfect,
he became the author of eternal salvation.*
HEBREWS 5:9 KJV

Not to Worry

When you choose to worry, you are choosing not to trust God.

You wouldn't rebuff someone who offered assistance if your car conked out on the highway. You wouldn't refuse a new neighbor who offers to help you move furniture out of the U-Haul into the new house. It would be an insult to say "No thanks" in these situations. So, if you wouldn't want to be impolite to strangers, why do you insult God by refusing His offer to relieve you of worries?

When you continue to worry about your problems, you are choosing to reject God's offer to comfort you. You are stubbornly holding on to your anxiety and foolishly declining God's help. Either you want to keep worrying, or you don't trust God.

Isn't it about time that you finally concede the fact that you can't handle your worries by yourself? Isn't it about time to accept the help and comfort that God offers?

---

*"So don't worry about having
enough food or drink or clothing. . . .
Your heavenly Father already knows all your needs,
and he will give you all you need from day to day if you live for
him and make the Kingdom of God your primary concern."*
MATTHEW 6:31–33

GOD IS IN THE BIG STUFF

Always be amazed at what God does, but never surprised.

Don't get discouraged when politics don't go the way you want them to. Get involved if you believe that's where God wants you, but don't get frustrated if things don't go your way. Never forget that God is in control, no matter who is in office (Rom. 13:1).

Pray for your leaders and do your part to improve your community. If you still have energy after that, ask God to use you to impact the hearts and minds of those who govern you. God has changed the tide of nations before, and there's no reason to believe He won't do it again.

Remember, when God's people pray, God listens, and He promises to "heal their land" (2 Chron. 7:14). We should never think that God can't work in the big stuff as well as the small. And when He does, we shouldn't be surprised.

There was great joy throughout the land
because the LORD had changed the attitude of
the king of Assyria toward them.
EZRA 6:22

What You Have Isn't Yours

Manage your money as if it belongs to God. (It does.)

As the twenty-two-year-old prepared to move out of his parents' home for life "on his own" across the country, he looked longingly around the house. All of his worldly possessions were packed in three boxes that fit in the trunk of the Neon, so he was beginning to covet all of the furniture, appliances, stereo equipment, and televisions. The refrigerator was well stocked (and all he had was an ice chest with two Snapples and a cheese sandwich). Finally he blurted out, "Why should I leave all of this?"

His father was quick to reply, "Because it isn't yours!"

Don't ever be stingy or possessive with what you own. "It isn't yours." Everything you have is on loan to you from God. Be as generous with your belongings as God would want you to be with His (because they are God's anyway).

The rich and the poor have this in common:
The LORD made them both.
PROVERBS 22:2

SHARING AND HOLDING BACK

Share your blessings with others,
but keep your whining to yourself.

Many of us are guilty of griping and complaining. We try to disguise our whining by categorizing it as "sharing our prayer requests," but we are really just looking for the opportunity to do a little groaning and grumbling.

There is nothing wrong with legitimate prayer requests. God wants us to share our prayer concerns with other believers. But don't dump your self-pity on someone else. When you do that, you're only looking for attention and sympathy. Your attitude needs to be changed more than your circumstances, and you are the only one who has control over that.

Whenever you are tempted to unload your gripes on someone, resist the urge. Instead, think of what you can say that will be encouraging. They'll benefit from what you have to say (and it will be good for you to dwell on positive things).

Though they have been going
through much trouble and hard times,
their wonderful joy and deep poverty
have overflowed in rich generosity.
2 CORINTHIANS 8:2

Is God Too Weak?

*Give God credit for the big stuff in the world
as well as the small stuff in your life.*

When something big and positive happens in the world, don't automatically chalk it up to human efforts or the work of nature. When you read about a major peace treaty between nations or growing prosperity in certain parts of the country, don't think that God isn't interested or involved.

A forest fire ravaged Yellowstone National Park some years ago, and people called it "an act of God." But now that the landscape and animals are back—more beautiful and plentiful than ever—people give the credit to "Mother Nature." Don't buy into that! It is God Who blesses His world, down to the tiniest flower (Matt. 6:30).

"Was I too weak to save you?" God asked (Isa. 50:2). Of course not! God is powerful enough to save a nation, and He is loving enough to save you.

---

*When our enemies and the surrounding nations heard about it,
they were frightened and humiliated.
They realized that this work had been done
with the help of our God.*
Nehemiah 6:16

WHAT MOTIVATES YOU?

*Let your primary motivation be the still,
small voice of the Holy Spirit.*

The advertising industry knows you very well. Billions of dollars have been invested in determining what impressions will motivate you to spend your hard-earned dollars. The television ads are written and directed to catch your attention. The magazine advertisements use the images that will capture your imagination. Whether it is the clothes you wear, or the car you drive, or a brand of deodorant, advertisers have determined that you are motivated by your self-image.

Self-image shouldn't be your motivating force if you belong to God. Your motivation should be to please and honor God (although that will never be one of the multiple-choice answers on a marketing survey). Don't get caught as part of the herd that moves according to the dictates of fashion and style. Let God be the image that determines your choices.

---

*"When the Spirit of truth comes,
he will guide you into all truth."*
JOHN 16:13

MADE FOR A PURPOSE

Live life on purpose, not by accident.

Knowing where you came from makes a huge difference in your life. Let's say you believed that you were the product of some cosmic accident. No intelligent design was involved in this world or your life. Things "just happened," and you just happen to be here. When you believe you got here by accident, you will live your life by accident. It may not seem like that to you, because you'll make your plans and set your goals, but for what overall purpose?

When you know without a doubt that God made the universe and created you in His image (Gen. 1:27), you know you were made for a purpose. God is very purposeful in what He does, from every small thing to each major event in your life. Imagine the confidence that gives you! Now move from imagining to believing. Believe that you can live your life on purpose because you were made for a purpose.

For we are God's masterpiece.
He has created us anew in Christ Jesus,
so that we can do the good things he planned for us long ago.
EPHESIANS 2:10

CARING IN ACTION

Make sure your caring includes doing.

Everyone usually looks so nice at church. The clothes are clean, the hair is combed, and the breath is fresh. This makes for a nice Norman Rockwell portrait, but it isn't God's intention for Christianity. Forget these notions of such a sterile environment. God wants you getting down and dirty as you help others.

If you really love God, you're going to get sweaty. It involves hard work. It means serving others (and we aren't just talking about pouring punch at the church picnic). Maybe God will want you to wash windows or mow the lawn at the home of someone who is ill or disabled. That trip to the beach might have to be postponed so you can help with chores at a village in Mexico during your vacation.

God is more pleased by seeing your dirty hands than your pressed apparel.

Pure and lasting religion in the sight of God our Father means that we must care for orphans and widows in their troubles, and refuse to let the world corrupt us.
JAMES 1:27

GOD IS PATIENT

God is willing to wait for you, but don't wait too long for Him.

Good things usually come when we are patient. Impatience usually leads to hasty decisions. And sometimes, when we are impatient, we miss out on the best possible result. God is never impatient because He always wants the best outcome. God sent Jesus into the world because He loved us. Because God has no other plan than Jesus to bring us into a right relationship with Him, He is willing to wait for us to respond.

God's divine patience means that each person will have the opportunity to accept the free gift of salvation through Jesus. But God won't wait forever. He has chosen the best possible moment to send Jesus back to Earth a second time. When that happens, time—like God's patience—will finally run out.

The Lord isn't really being slow about his promise to return,
as some people think.
No, he is being patient for your sake.
He does not want anyone to perish,
so he is giving more time for everyone to repent.
2 PETER 3:9

GREATNESS

*True greatness is measured by the things you do
for people who can't reciprocate.*

Quid *pro quo* is a legal term that lawyers use to mean an equal exchange of consideration. Non-lawyers don't have to use Latin phrases. They can just say, "Even Stephen." You might also know this concept by its anatomical terminology, "You scratch my back, and I'll scratch yours."

There is nothing wrong with doing something for someone who can reciprocate. But there is nothing great about it, either. Don't think that you have the attitude of a humble servant when you offer to do a favor for someone if you have a "Now he owes me one" mentality.

Look for things that you can do for someone who has no ability to repay you. When you aren't concerned about keeping things equal, then you'll be acting like a humble servant.

*"And anyone who welcomes a little child like this
on my behalf is welcoming me."*
MATTHEW 18:5

THE DANGER OF KNOWLEDGE

When you think you've learned enough, you haven't.

You'll never come to the point where you know enough about God. Knowing God is a lifelong pursuit that grows more rewarding as you learn more. It's not like studying physics or seventeenth-century British poets, where you get to the point of saying, "I've had enough!" Learning about God brings you peace (because you know He is in control), joy (because you know He wants the best for you), and a desire to know God better.

There is a danger in knowledge, however. You can substitute what you know about God objectively for actually knowing God personally. You aren't Sherlock Holmes, and God doesn't belong under a magnifying glass. He belongs in your heart, where He can change you into the person He wants you to be, reflecting His glory to others.

Fear of the LORD is the beginning of knowledge.
PROVERBS 1:7

HANDLING MONEY

Let money be your servant, not your master.

The more you have, the more you have to lose. So, you purchase insurance. But the more insurance you have, the higher the premiums are. To afford the higher premiums, you try to make a little more income. With more income, your taxes are higher. To cover increased taxes, you buy some rental property. Now you need more insurance. And so it goes.

There is a vicious cycle involved with money. Don't get caught in it. Keep your desires in check. If you feel compelled to match the acquisitions of your friends and neighbors, you will be in a race that has no finish line.

Let God help you establish an acceptable standard of living for your circumstances. If He gives you financial blessings that would allow you to raise your lifestyle a notch or two, then think about giving away the excess before you automatically spend it on yourself.

Don't weary yourself trying to get rich.
Why waste your time?
For riches can disappear as though
they had the wings of a bird!
PROVERBS 23:4–5

AN OFFER YOU CAN'T REFUSE

*You can acquire wisdom over time,
but God promises to give it to you if you ask.*

W hat would you do if God offered you anything
you wanted? What would you ask for? God posed this question to Solomon, the son of King David and a king in his own
right. How did Solomon respond? He asked for "an understanding mind" (1 Kings 3:9). To say God answered His
request is an understatement. History records that Solomon
was the wisest man who ever lived (for a sampling of his wise
words, read the Book of Proverbs).

Would you ask God for wisdom above all else? It
seems like a pretty good idea. Now, God probably won't give
you the same kind of wisdom He gave Solomon, but He has
made you the same offer: He will give you wisdom if you ask
for it. It's not like you're suddenly going to get super smart.
But you will find that as you gain wisdom, you will begin to
see things from God's perspective.

---

*If you need wisdom—
if you want to know what God wants you to do—
ask him, and he will gladly tell you.*
JAMES 1:5

WHAT IS YOUR
RESPONSE-ABILITY?

What happens to you may be an accident.
How you respond is not.

Perspective is everything. A toddler cries when the stack of blocks falls over. (The parent knows that this is no big deal.) A child quits when the peewee baseball team loses a game. (The parent knows that this loss will soon be forgotten.) And the teenaged guy feels rejected if he isn't invited to the Sadie Hawkins dance. (We can speak from personal experience on this one. Life does go on.)

Change *your* perspective. Look at circumstances from God's point of view. If you have an eternal perspective, then all of your difficulties will seem to shrink. God doesn't see insurmountable obstacles in your life, although they may appear that way to you. He is able to conquer any adverse situation, so look at it through His eyes. Before you know it, the problem will be gone, and the unpleasantness will be forgotten.

Yet I will rejoice in the LORD!
I will be joyful in the God of my salvation.
HABAKKUK 3:18

THE RIGHT THING

*If you aren't learning to do the right thing,
you aren't acquiring wisdom.*

The dictionary defines wisdom as "knowledge and good judgment based on experience." That sounds good, but what if your experiences aren't so good? What if you make some bad choices that lead to some negative experiences? About the only wisdom you can acquire is the wisdom not to do that stuff again!

Hey, we've all been there, so we all have to ask ourselves, "How do we get the wisdom to do what's right? Where do we begin?"

Here's Solomon's advice: "Fear of the Lord is the beginning of wisdom" (Prov. 9:10). That doesn't mean we are afraid of God. As Chuck Swindoll says, to fear God means to "take Him seriously and do what He says." When you do what God says, you do what's right. And when you do what's right, you are wise.

---

*Those who are wise will find
a time and a way to do what is right.*
ECCLESIASTES 8:5

WHAT IS REALLY FUNNY?

*A true sense of humor does not rely on
the humiliation of others.*

We all like to make people laugh. It is rewarding to bring levity into someone's life. And the ability to make people laugh will get you invited to a lot of parties because people with a good sense of humor are fun to have around.

Unfortunately, some people try too hard to be funny. In their attempt, they go for the "cheap shot" instead of a humorous comment. There is laughter at both, but the cheap shot usually involves making fun at someone's expense. Maybe it is a sarcastic remark about an expanding waistline, or a receding hairline.

Christians should be the happiest group of people. They should be laughing all of the time. But their jokes should never be made at the expense of someone's feelings.

*Instead, be kind to each other, tenderhearted,
forgiving one another,
just as God through Christ has forgiven you.*
EPHESIANS 4:32

SPIRITUAL DISCERNMENT

Seeing is better than looking.
Listening is better than hearing.
Doing is better than talking.

There are a lot of advantages to being a Christian. The biggest advantage is that you know you are going to spend eternity with God. But being a Christian is more than having an eternal fire insurance policy. It means you can live your life with a clearer understanding of yourself and others (it's called *discernment*).

As a Christian, you have spiritual discernment, thanks to the presence of the Holy Spirit in your life (1 Cor. 2:12). Now, it's possible for someone without God to be wise in the ways of the world, but when it comes to spiritual matters, they are in a fog (1 Cor. 2:14). See what an advantage you have? As long as you ask God for wisdom—and then you really see, listen, and do what is right—you will accomplish amazing things for God.

For if you just listen and don't obey,
it is like looking at your face in a mirror
but doing nothing to improve your appearance.
JAMES 1:23

PRAYER PREVAILS

Prayer changes things, but worry changes nothing.

Worry usually results when you have exhausted all of your options. When you have done everything possible—when there is nothing left that you can do—then you worry if the problem still exists. Well, stop worrying. There is one last step that you can take: You can pray.

Don't withhold your prayers until everything else fails. (Your first step in tackling a problem should be to pray about it.) But you'll never hit the proverbial brick wall if you remember to pray your way through it.

We are the first to admit that prayer doesn't always change the circumstances immediately, but it can change you rather quickly. When you talk to God, He'll give you peace in the midst of your problems, and you'll be better able to keep working on the problem (while God does, too). But don't take our word for it, take His.

Don't worry about anything;
instead, pray about everything.
Tell God what you need,
and thank him for all he has done.
PHILIPPIANS 4:6

SIDE BY SIDE

*It's easier to communicate face-to-face
if you're walking side by side.*

Ohe of the best ways to communicate with someone is to walk side by side. When you face another person, there's that issue of eye contact to deal with. When you're in front of someone, you can't see his face, and when you're behind, he can't see yours. No, side by side is the best. You're together, going in the same direction. When someone comes alongside, you gain confidence and courage.

That's the picture of how God relates to us. He sent Jesus to die for us, but after He rose from the dead, Jesus returned to heaven, where He is on our side by pleading for us before the Father (1 John 2:1). And right here on Earth, the Holy Spirit comes alongside us as our Counselor and Comforter (John 14:16).

---

*"And I will ask the Father,
and he will give you another Counselor,
who will never leave you."*
JOHN 14:16

GOSSIP

Gossip should never be disguised as concern.

You know that gossip should be avoided. So, you wouldn't schedule a weekly meeting at Starbucks with a few friends for a gossip session. But there is a risk that the same thing could happen with as much regularity at many churches (and coffee is even served). We're talking about "prayer meetings."

There is temptation to gossip when you are sharing "prayer requests" about other people. It is easy to let your concern shift to conjecture. Instead of sharing requests, you can find yourself sharing rumors.

Satan knows that prayers are effective. He will try to get you distracted from thoughts of God's sovereignty and focused more on people's scandal.

What dainty morsels rumors are—
but they sink deep into one's heart.
PROVERBS 26:22

ARE YOU PREJUDICED?

*The only way to rid yourself of prejudice
is to see people through the eyes of Jesus.*

Prejudice is the barrier that keeps one person from accepting another. Racial prejudice is an obvious example, but there are many cultural, economic, and social prejudices as well. Whatever the distinction, if it creates a barrier between you and others, then you may be struggling with prejudice.

Jesus was unaffected by racial, social, and cultural barriers. He wanted to share His message about God's love with everyone. That is why He ignored social differences and began talking with the Samaritan woman, who not only had a bad reputation but was also a member of a despised race (John 4:4–26). He ignored economic and moral differences when He visited the home of Zacchaeus (Luke 19:1–10).

Let Jesus be your example. Stop looking at the differences between yourself and others. See people through the eyes of Jesus, as those who need to know God's love.

---

*Doesn't this discrimination show that
you are guided by wrong motives?*
JAMES 2:4

WHAT'S YOUR CHOICE?

When it comes to eternity,
seats are available in the smoking and the non-smoking sections.
Which do you prefer?

Eternity is serious business because it never ends. Where you will spend eternity is your own choice. (God doesn't send anyone to hell; they go there because they reject His free offer of salvation.) Since it is up to you, make sure you have chosen wisely—and failing to choose is a choice in itself.

If you haven't made up your mind yet, here is a thought that might be of help: For Christians, life on this earth is as close as they will ever get to hell. For people who reject God, life on this earth is as close to heaven as they will ever get. (If you already belong to God, then read those last two sentences over again whenever you are getting weary of this world. For you, the best is yet to come.)

"Everyone who believes in me
will have eternal life."
JOHN 3:15

GOD ISN'T IN OUR IMAGE

You wouldn't want to know a God invented by people.

The Bible tells us that God made the world and created people in His image (Gen. 1:1, 27). Apparently that isn't good enough for the human race. The world has turned the tables and has created God in its image.

What if that were actually true? What if God had human characteristics and acted like people do? At first people would be thrilled. Their designer God wouldn't judge them, and He wouldn't be involved in their world. God would be whatever they wanted Him to be. But then the thrill would turn to horror as people did whatever seemed right in their own eyes (Judg. 17:6).

We should thank God that He isn't in our image. He isn't like us and doesn't act the way we do. He doesn't lie, He doesn't change, He doesn't judge unfairly, and He doesn't love conditionally. He is God, and above Him there is no other.

"God is not a man, that he should lie.
He is not a human, that he should change his mind.
Has he ever spoken and failed to act?
Has he ever promised and not carried it through?"
NUMBERS 23:19

DIVERSITY

*Appreciate the diversities in other people
instead of criticizing them.*

The apostle Paul preached and wrote about the subject of diversity long before the topic became politically correct. Diversity was an issue in the first-century churches. Those early Christian churches were composed of Jews and Gentiles, the rich and the slaves, the educated and the illiterate. In the context of these widespread differences, Paul urged unity.

Paul's message is just as relevant today. Within the same church, there can be believers who come from different cultural or economic backgrounds. These differences are irrelevant to God, so they should not be a basis of division for the rest of us. And Paul's message isn't limited to individual churches. It applies to all believers, with whom there will be significant diversity in worship styles and the formality (or lack thereof) in their respective services.

If we learn to value each other as God sees us, our differences will not be divisive.

*Always keep yourselves united in the Holy Spirit,
and bind yourselves together with peace.*
EPHESIANS 4:3

DO GOD'S THING

*The reason God wants us to do things His way is
because it's the best way.*

Do your own thing" may be a catchy slogan, but it's a lousy philosophy. God is all for us being unique—after all, He made no two of us alike—but He's not in favor of our putting our own interests first.

We humans have a history of doing our own thing, usually with disastrous results. It's called rebellion against God. When people reject God's way of doing things and choose their own, they reject a perfect plan in favor of a corrupt path. Just look at Adam and Eve, the first parents. They had paradise at their disposal. That was God's perfect plan for them. Yet they chose their own way, leading to a very bad outcome.

Every day we are faced with choices, most of which come back to the same question. Do we want to do things our way or God's way?

---

*In those days Israel had no king,
so the people did whatever seemed right in their own eyes.*
JUDGES 17:6

FAULTS

If you make an effort to overlook the little faults in others,
maybe they'll do the same with your glaring flaws.

It is easier to see the faults in other people. We can quickly identify the problems in someone else's life. Maybe it is a shrill voice, or an annoying habit. Other people may lack good manners or speak with poor grammar. Some are just plain losers. Then there are those people who are critical of others (they are the worst). Aren't you glad the rest of us are so perfect?

We hope you detected a note of sarcasm in the last paragraph. (More than a note, it was a whole tune.) Yes, you can always find faults with other people. Nobody is perfect. But if you are interested in honing your critical skills, you should start with yourself. Don't move on to others until you have completely identified all of your shortcomings and corrected each of them. (That should keep you busy for a lifetime.)

"How can you think of saying,
'Let me help you get rid of that speck in your eye,'
when you can't see past the log in your own eye? Hypocrite!
First get rid of the log from your own eye;
then perhaps you will see well enough to deal with
the speck in your friend's eye."
MATTHEW 7:4–5

WORD POWER

Develop your vocabulary, not to impress others,
but to bless them.

Words are amazingly versatile. They can be destructive weapons, or they can be agents of peace. Words can kill, and words can heal. Every day we make choices as to how we are going to use our words, or at least we should. Too often we speak before we think. We throw our words out there carelessly rather than thoughtfully, and once they're out there, we can't take them back.

We can do better! It's not just a matter of thinking before we speak (although that's a great place to start). We need to build our vocabulary to include those words that edify and encourage others. The negative words come all too naturally (because that's mainly what we hear), but positive words take work. You also have to know the person you're encouraging so your words don't seem like insincere flattery.

Kind words are like honey—
sweet to the soul and healthy for the body.
PROVERBS 16:24

A GOOD INVESTMENT

*Spend more of your time and energy investing in people
than you do investing in things.*

A good investment is determined by the safety of
your capital and the rate of return. If you are going to put your
money into something, you want to make sure that it won't be
lost and that you'll be paid a good dividend.

These same principles apply to the investment of your
time and energy. Don't waste your valuable time with frivolous
endeavors. Put your effort where it will count and pay off. You
may receive the best return on your investment when you put
time into other people. You can invest in them through acts of
kindness and thoughtfulness. You aren't likely to see monetary
returns on your investment, but you are guaranteed spiritual
rewards because your good deeds honor God Himself.

---

*Don't just pretend that you love others.
Really love them. Hate what is wrong.
Stand on the side of the good.
Love each other with genuine affection,
and take delight in honoring each other.*
ROMANS 12:9–10

GUARD YOUR HEART

*What you get out of your body directly relates to
what you put into it.*

These days we are very aware of the benefits of healthful foods and the negative effects of unhealthy foods on our bodies. That doesn't mean we eat right all the time, but at least we know how.

If all you had to worry about was keeping your physical body healthy, then you could concentrate completely on the food you put into your mouth. But your body has a spiritual dimension as well, and you can easily feed it with unhealthful sights and sounds. If you deliberately listen to negative words and words that contradict what God wants for you, then negative things are going to come out of you. If you choose to view unhealthful sights, your spiritual body will suffer. Above all else, guard your ears and your eyes. Just as your mouth is the gateway to your body, they are the gateways to your heart.

------

*"Your eye is a lamp for your body.
A pure eye lets sunshine into your soul."*
MATTHEW 6:22

WHAT'S LEFT AFTER DEATH?

*Be more concerned with the legacy you'll leave to your children
than the inheritance you'll receive from your parents.*

Your tombstone is likely to be engraved with the year of your birth and the year of your death (such as 1948–2027). On that grave marker, the sum of your life will be represented by the hyphen that separates the two dates. But the impact of your life is not relegated to the etchings on a tombstone. The heritage that you leave behind will be the influence you had on others.

Many people worry about the assets that they will leave for their children. But assets can be squandered, or lost, or stolen. Wouldn't you prefer to leave your friends and family with something of eternal, everlasting value? Leave them an example of a life committed to God. Let your legacy be a reverence for God.

------

*I could have no greater joy than to hear
that my children live in the truth.*
3 JOHN 4

LIVING THE TRUTH

*You can't claim to be living in the light if
you are walking in darkness.*

It is easy to get absorbed with religious lingo and forget what it really means. For example, we use a phrase like "living in the light" without remembering its significance. Without pretending to explain the meaning in full, here are three practical aspects for you to remember:

- Living in the light involves consistent conduct: behaving in a manner that is pleasing to God.
- Living in the light involves transformed thinking: making decisions based on God's wisdom instead of your own.
- Living in the light involves purpose: being motivated by God to work for His Kingdom.

Meditate on the meaning of what you read in Scripture. What you read should change the way you think. How you think should change the way you live.

---

*If we are living in the light of God's presence,
just as Christ is, then we have fellowship with each other,
and the blood of Jesus, his Son, cleanses us from every sin.*
1 JOHN 1:7

YOU ARE GOD'S HOUSE

God expects you to keep your house in order.

Did you know that God considers you to be a dwelling? That's right, in a very real spiritual sense, you are a "house of God." You begin your relationship with God by inviting Jesus into your house. Jesus says, "Here I am! I stand at the door and knock. If anyone hears my voice and opens the door, I will come in and eat with him, and he with me" (Rev. 3:20 NIV). Once you invite Jesus in, the Holy Spirit takes up residence in your body, which is like a "temple" for God (1 Cor. 6:19).

Like any house, your body needs maintenance. If your body is left unattended, it will get dirty and decay. But you should never build up your physical house at the expense of your spiritual one. You are the house of God, and as long as He is going to live there, He expects you to take care of His place.

———————

"Why are you living in luxurious houses
while my house lies in ruins?"
HAGGAI 1:4

FAMILY TIES

Friendships can fade, but families are forever.

We live in a mobile society where it is easy to become disconnected from your family. No longer do three generations live in the same house on a farm. (Even John Boy eventually moved away from Walton's Mountain.) It seems that the farther we live from each other, the more distant our relationships become.

But there doesn't have to be a proportional relationship between distance and family connectedness. Sure, you might have to work a little harder at it (because you aren't eating dinner at the same table), but it is possible to stay close while you are far apart.

Take advantage of the Internet and send E-mail to your family members regularly. (Or if you are a traditionalist, then put a postage stamp on an envelope.) Stay in touch with your family. They need to know that you care.

But those who won't care for their own relatives,
especially those living in the same household,
have denied what we believe.
Such people are worse than unbelievers.
1 TIMOTHY 5:8

The Love of Money

Money can do a lot of things,
and one of the things it does best is take your eyes off God.

There are lots of things you should pray for, but money isn't one of them. Pray for God's provision, but don't pray for riches. It isn't that money is wrong. Money is neutral. The Bible doesn't say, "Money is the root of all evil." It's "the love of money is at the root of all kinds of evil" (1 Tim. 6:10). The problem isn't money, but our desire for it. Friendships end, marriages break apart, crimes are committed, and people stay away from God—all over money.

Money is one of the "big three" temptations for the Christian, especially if you are in a position of leadership (the other two are sex and power). Money is a weak spot for us, and Satan knows it. Count on him to attack and entice you with the almighty dollar. That's why you need to count on Almighty God to help you keep your eyes on Him.

"You cannot serve both God and money."
LUKE 16:13

Cetaphil Cleanser, soap
+ moisturizer

This complimentary prescription pad has been produced for you by

In the event your practice information has changed, or if your supply of pads runs low (4 weeks' supply left,) please mail the pink reorder card or the reorder sheet with your changes to:

Triple i
Customer Service Center
P.O. Box 7431
West Trenton, NJ 08628-0431

Call or Fax Toll-Free:
Call: 1-800-969-7237
Fax: 1-800-233-9141

THE LURE OF SEX

Sex is God's wedding gift to the bride and groom.

It would be easy to think that sexual sin is the worse kind of sin, but that's not true. All sin is equally bad in God's eyes (it's all a violation of His perfect standard and His will for us). However, we may be more susceptible to sexual sin than other sins, because it can invade our thoughts as well as our bodies (Matt. 5:28).

Of course, you can get physically sick as a result of sexual sin. But don't think that just because you are disease-free, you're off the hook. God designed sex for marriage, and anything else degrades your relationship with Him. It infects your thoughts and drives out the effectiveness of the Holy Spirit in your life. That's why God doesn't want us to be passive about sexual temptation. He wants us to run the other way.

Run away from sexual sin!
No other sin so clearly affects the body as this one does.
1 CORINTHIANS 6:18

THE LONGING FOR POWER

Embrace the power of love. Reject the love of power.

The last of the "big three" temptations is power. From your position as a student or laborer or office manager or pastor, you may feel that power will never tempt you. Think again.

Jesus came to Earth as a servant (Phil. 2:7). The prophet Isaiah wrote that Jesus was "despised and rejected—a man of sorrows" (Isa. 53:3). If anyone was immune to the temptation of power, it was Jesus. Yet that's exactly where Satan tempted Him. He offered Jesus the world if only Jesus would kneel down and worship him (Matt. 4:9).

Satan used that tactic on Jesus, and you can be sure he will use it on you. The only way you can resist is to do what Jesus did. Tell Satan to take a hike, and rely on the Word of God.

"Get out of here, Satan," Jesus told him.
"For the Scriptures say,
'You must worship the Lord your God;
serve only him.'"
MATTHEW 4:10

FRIENDSHIPS FIT TOGETHER

*The best way to compensate for your weaknesses is
to find a friend who has strengths in those areas.*

Friends can be useful. If you are moving to a new
apartment, you need friends to help you pack up the boxes
and lift the furniture. If you are traveling across the country,
you need a free place to stay. (Or is that what relatives are for?)
But the value of friendship is more than a matter of convenience. It is a matter of completeness.

You are a person with strengths and weaknesses. Your
friends can complement your weak areas. Although you have
much in common with your friends, they will have perspec-
tives and opinions that are different from yours. As a team of
two or more, you can be more effective than any of you could
be individually.

Take time to thank the Lord for your friends. Then
call a few of your friends and thank them for their friendships.

---

*A person standing alone can be attacked and defeated,
but two can stand back-to-back and conquer.
Three are even better,
for a triple-braided cord is not easily broken.*
ECCLESIASTES 4:12

WHAT TO DO WITH
WHAT YOU HEAR

Be quick to receive the truth when someone corrects you,
and be quicker to dismiss the gossip about someone else.

It's easy to get distracted from what you should be thinking about. You can start the day by reading the Bible and meditating on a few spiritual thoughts. But during the course of the day, someone will say something that offends you (and then you'll have resentful thoughts), or you'll hear a rumor (and get caught in the snare of gossip). It is a constant struggle to keep your mind on the things of God. Moving to a monastery isn't an option for most of us, so you'll have to learn to manage your thoughts.

If you hear a personal criticism, don't overreact. While some of the comment may be false, there just might be a shred of truth in there. Maybe you can learn and improve from it. And if you hear a criticism of someone else, don't dwell on it. When your mind strays, refocus on God.

Fix your thoughts on what is true and honorable and right.
Think about things that are pure and lovely and admirable.
Think about things that are excellent and worthy of praise.
PHILIPPIANS 4:8

REJECT REJECTION

A person has yet to be born who is worthy of rejection.

One of the main reasons we pass judgment on people is for the purpose of rejecting them. We want them out of our sight and out of our mind. So we judge them, reject them, and move on to another victim. That sounds terrible, and yet we're all guilty of seeing people that way, even people we've never met.

Here's a way to get out of the ugly cycle of judgment and rejection. Whenever you meet people, whether you know them or not, try to see them the way Jesus does. Don't try to figure out if they love God (that's not for you to judge!). Instead, see others as people Jesus loves so much that He died for them. If you begin to see people in this way, not only will you accept them, but you may also be used by God to share the Good News of God's love with them.

Yes indeed, it is good when you truly obey
our Lord's royal command found in the Scriptures:
"Love your neighbor as yourself."
JAMES 2:8

PRIDE

Pride is like body odor:
Everyone notices except the person who has it.

Pride can affect your perspective. When you have a prideful attitude, you start looking down on other people instead of looking inward at your own faults. A prideful spirit has you looking at yourself instead of looking up toward God.

Pride in ourselves, in our possessions, or in our accomplishments is a slap in God's face. Our pride means that we are taking credit for what God has given to us. Or, it ignores our own sins and overlooks the grace of God's forgiveness.

Instead of pride, we should be humble before God and grateful for His mercy to us. When we remember Who God is, and if we have an accurate understanding of who we are in comparison, we have nothing to be prideful about.

If we are living now by the Holy Spirit,
let us follow the Holy Spirit's leading in every part of our lives.
Let us not become conceited.
GALATIANS 5:25–26

FALSELY ACCUSED

There's no dishonor in being falsely accused;
it happens to the best of us.

Being falsely accused is difficult to handle. In fact, it may be one of the most difficult personal obstacles you will ever face—and you will face it. If you don't believe that, think about Jesus. He faced accusations that contained no shred of truth. He was brought before the great religious and political leaders of His day and falsely accused of many charges. Jesus could have defended Himself, but He was silent. Why?

Jesus was willing to let His life speak for itself. He knew that God would vindicate Him. When others try to discredit you, are you willing to let God defend you? If you are falsely accused and suffer for doing right, don't assume you are the only one who can protect and defend your reputation. Do what Jesus did and trust that God will take care of the situation.

For we know the one who said,
"I will take vengeance. I will repay those who deserve it."
HEBREWS 10:30

SPECIAL FAVOR

Be glad that your salvation doesn't depend on you,
because you aren't good enough.

Jesus did more than show us a better way to live. He abolished the need for rules—there is no standard of conduct by which we are measured. By sacrificing His life for us, He did us a "special favor." He made it possible for us to satisfy God's perfect standard by His forgiveness rather than on our own performance.

Don't fall into the trap of hanging on to the old rules as a way of satisfying God. Don't think that by doing everything right, you'll be good enough for God. You can't do it, so don't even try. Make no mistake about it. Righteous living pleases God, but the only way to gain salvation is to accept the forgiveness that is available through Jesus.

Your lifestyle should be in response to God's love, not an attempt to win His love.

"We believe that we are all saved the same way,
by the special favor of the Lord Jesus."
ACTS 15:11

THE SIMPLE LIFE

While the poor dream of having riches,
the wealthy long for simplicity.

Lottery fever is sweeping the country. The lure of "get rich quick" dangles at the end of everyone's line. What a hopeless illusion. Never mind that you have a greater chance of getting struck by lightning while standing on your head in a bowl of corn flakes than of winning the lottery. Quick riches never did anyone any good. They certainly never brought anyone happiness.

We've never been rich, so how do we know that? Simple. We've never heard anyone say, "I'm rich, and finally I'm happy." Instead we've heard stuff like "Wealth is, a burden," or "I wish my life were a lot simpler." The truth is, wealth can do a lot (both good and bad), but it complicates your life. There's nothing wrong with wealth (and neither is there any dishonor in poverty). What matters is your contentment with what you have.

We are merely moving shadows,
and all our busy rushing ends in nothing.
We heap up wealth for someone else to spend.
PSALM 39:6

No Worries

Worrying occurs when God is left out of the process.

Worry isn't a verb; it's an emotion. We know that, yet we act as if it isn't true. We think that if we worry enough, our circumstances are going to change. We think we can worry things and events into existence. Doesn't that sound silly? We ought to be embarrassed over how much faith we put in worry, and we need to wake up to the real problem. When we worry, we make a choice not to trust God. In effect, we tell God that He's not interested in us or capable of helping us.

God has made it very clear that He is very interested in us and very capable of helping us. He may not help us instantly (which is part of the reason we skip past God and start to worry), but He will help us in His time. Give your cares to God, give your problems to God, and most of all, give your worries to God.

Give all your worries and cares to God,
for he cares about what happens to you.
1 PETER 5:7

PREPARING FOR BATTLE

Most Christians spend more time getting ready for church than they spend getting prepared to battle Satan.

A good soldier is prepared for warfare. He goes into the battle with protective battle gear and armed with weapons.

As a Christian, you are engaged in a spiritual battle. Satan is doing everything he can to prevent you from living a victorious life. He wants to deceive, discourage, and distract you from growing closer to God.

You can't withstand Satan's attacks by yourself, so God has provided battle gear for your protection and weapons for your use. He wants you to be adequately armed and protected from the attacks of Satan.

Read about spiritual armor in Ephesians 6:10–18. Notice that there is no protection for your back. You won't need it. With God on your side, you will never have to run away from Satan in defeat.

Put on all of God's armor so that you will be able to stand firm against all strategies and tricks of the Devil.
EPHESIANS 6:11

HANDLING TEMPTATION

It is easier to resist temptation if you don't go looking for it.

There is nothing wrong with temptation. Until you give in to it, you haven't done anything wrong. You still have the option of doing what is right.

For some people, resisting temptation isn't a problem because they don't try to. They simply do *what* they want, *when* they want. But if you're going to attempt to live a life that is pleasing to God, you need to learn how to handle temptation.

You'll never successfully resist temptation if you try to do it in your own power. It will happen only with God's power in your life through the Holy Spirit.

If you have been discouraged by your failure to resist temptation, then give up. Stop trying to do something that you know is futile. But don't give in. Depend on God for the power to resist. Focus on Him instead of the temptation.

And God is faithful.
He will keep the temptation from becoming
so strong that you can't stand up against it.
When you are tempted,
he will show you a way out so that you will not give in to it.
1 CORINTHIANS 10:13

IF NOT US, WHO?

Trust God to direct the circumstances of your life
even if you don't know what He's doing.

In a time of crisis, an American president gave this charge to the nation: "If not now, when? If not us, who?" It was an inspiring phrase, but not original. The Bible records an event in 479 B.C., when a beautiful Jewish woman named Esther became queen of Persia. It was no accident. God arranged the circumstances of her life in order to elevate her to a high position, and then He used her to save His people.

Whenever you are promoted to a higher position—whether it's in your job, at school, or in the community—you need to recognize that God has put you there for a reason. You may not know right away, but you have to trust God that His timing is perfect, and you need to stay humble with the knowledge that He wants to use you to serve and influence others and glorify Him.

"What's more, who can say but that you have been elevated
to the palace for just such a time as this?"
ESTHER 4:14

YOUR VALUES

Most people treat their values like a piece of furniture—
they move it around if it gets in their way.

Humans are good at making rules. Our country has rules, our states and cities have rules, and even families make their own rules. Deciding on the rules is not a problem, but keeping them is.

The same thing could be said about values. There is no shortage of discussion about them. But talking about them isn't doing much good. The problem is living them.

God is calling you to live according to a set of principles, but they are of a higher level than society's rules and values. Society's set of principles stops at your door and allows you to do whatever you want in your private life. That's not the way it is in God's divine plan. He wants you to live according to His holiness, and He wants you to apply that standard to both your public and private life.

God has called us to be holy, not to live impure lives.
Anyone who refuses to live by these rules is not
disobeying human rules but is rejecting God,
who gives his Holy Spirit to you.
1 THESSALONIANS 4:7–8

Dream On

Don't let your dreams die.

It's in our nature to dream. There are the dreams you dream when you're asleep (by the way, have you ever noticed that you dream a lot more when you're rested?). And there are the dreams you dream when you're awake. Let's talk about your daydreams for a minute.

When your daydreams drift to fantasy worlds and unrealistic results, they're pretty useless. But when you use your dreams to focus on something better for yourself and others, they can be very motivating. One big dream every Christian should have centers on the stuff God has prepared for us beyond this life on Earth (1 Cor. 2:9). This is not a fantasy land (although the mansions and gold streets may seem like that). Heaven is for real. When you dream of heaven, you are dreaming of something very realistic. This should give you tremendous motivation to serve God on Earth and love Him with your whole being.

---

*What is faith? It is the confident assurance that
what we hope for is going to happen.
It is the evidence of things we cannot yet see.*
HEBREWS 11:1

Talk about Forever

There is no way to get people out of hell,
but we should make every effort to keep them from going there.

Heaven isn't something from a fairy tale. It's a very real place that Jesus is preparing for those who have put their faith in Him. It is a place that will have no tears, pain, sorrow, or death. It is the hope of all you believe in Christ.

The Bible makes it very clear that unbelievers have a very different future. The descriptions of hell as a "lake of fire" and a "place of torment" give us a clue that it will be a terrible place.

Given the two alternatives, the choice is clear. You may have already made your decision, but there are many people who haven't. Since Christ died to keep people out of hell, can't you at least make some effort to talk with your friends and family about this most important choice?

"Their doom is in the lake that burns
with fire and sulfur.
This is the second death."
REVELATION 21:8

GOD WILL NEVER LEAVE YOU

God is in the business of helping, not hurting us.

One of the greatest fears we have is abandonment. As a baby, you probably cried when your mother left the room. As a youngster, you may have been left behind accidentally, or maybe you got separated in a crowd. Although your parents didn't mean it, you felt abandoned, and the uneasiness remains with you to this day.

As an adult, you don't fear being abandoned physically as much as you hate the idea of emotional abandonment. None of us wants to be left alone during times of need or crisis, but it happens. You may even feel as though God has abandoned you at times. What you need to realize is that can never happen. It may seem that God is far away at times, but the reality is that He is always right beside you. When those feelings of abandonment come, rest on the promises of God's Word.

For the Lord does not abandon anyone forever.
Though he brings grief,
he also shows compassion according to
the greatness of his unfailing love.
For he does not enjoy hurting people or causing them sorrow.
LAMENTATIONS 3:31–33

HUMILITY

*Humility is like underwear—
you should have it, but you shouldn't be proud of it.*

Humility is subtle. The moment you think you have it, you've lost it. Humility is not something you can strive for. It comes by learning to be submissive. One of the most difficult things for a proud person to do is to submit to someone else. But submission isn't difficult for someone who is humble.

God wants you to be humble. A spirit of arrogance is at odds with godly living. You can move toward humility if you remain submissive to God's leading. Don't try to assert yourself against His will. If you need a picture of humility, think of Christ. He humbled Himself by leaving heaven to come to Earth for your sake. It was a supreme act of humility for Him to take on human form when He was God's own Son.

There is another subtlety about humility. If you are humble before God, He will honor you.

---

*"God sets himself against the proud,
but he shows favor to the humble."
So humble yourselves under the mighty power of God,
and in his good time he will honor you.*
1 PETER 5:5–6

Start Trusting

Live longer by worrying less.

Worry is a double-edged sword. Not only is worry incapable of adding anything to your life, but it can also take things away from your life:

- *Health*—Worry leads to stress, which damages you physically.
- *Time*—The time you spend worrying takes away from the time you spend on other things.
- *Productivity*—When you spend less time on other things, your productivity drops.
- *Faith*—You can't worry and have faith at the same time.

The only way to add to your life is to stop worrying and start trusting.

"Can all your worries add a single moment to your life? Of course not."
MATTHEW 6:27

MERCY

The foolish person wants what he deserves;
the wise person knows better than to ask for it.

Mercy simply means not getting what you deserve. In a court of law, a judge can show mercy only to someone already declared guilty. Because we have violated God's perfect standard, we have been declared guilty and there's nothing we can do about it. We're at the mercy of the Judge of heaven. God showed us His mercy by sending His Son to take the punishment we deserved.

God's mercy to us is an example that we should follow by showing mercy to others. The next time you feel like retaliating at someone who has offended you, remember the mercy that God extended to you.

But that is why God had mercy on me,
so that Christ Jesus could use me as a prime example of
his great patience with even the worst sinners.
1 TIMOTHY 1:16

GOD WANTS YOUR PROBLEMS

Let your difficulties be opportunities for God's control.

Just about every problem you worry about is outside your control, which gives you the perfect opportunity to give your problems to God. Do you have a health issue you're dealing with, and there's nothing the doctors can do? Give your health to God. Do you lack confidence for that upcoming test, even though you've studied all you can? Give your test to God. Is your boss making life miserable for you despite your best efforts? Give your job to God.

At their worst, problems cause us to worry. At their best, problems test our faith. Do we trust God enough to let Him control everything in our lives? Are we willing to give Him our big problems as well as the small stuff? He's willing to take control of our difficulties if we just let Him.

But God will use this persecution to show his justice.
· 2 THESSALONIANS 1:5

FINDING A TRUE FRIEND

Select friends based on their character,
not their compliments.

When you were young, you didn't have much choice about your friends. They were probably the other kids who lived on your block. Since your parents made the housing decisions, you got what came with the neighborhood. Even as you got older, your friends at school were determined in large part by the classes that you had. (Again, you had little input in the whole matter.)

You are now at a stage when you get to select your own friends. Don't let it happen by default. Be very intentional about it. Look for friends that will raise you up to a higher level; avoid the people who would pull you down to theirs.

———————

As iron sharpens iron, a friend sharpens a friend.
PROVERBS 27:17

THE WORRY SUBSTITUTE

The best way to stop worrying is to start praying.

It's hard to stop worrying. Although we've never smoked, we can imagine that it's just as difficult to stop worrying as it is to stop smoking. Both activities are a form of addiction. Even though the habit is harmful to you, you can't help but engage in the activity.

So what's the best way to stop? With smoking, the experts say that rather than quit "cold turkey," you have to substitute something else—a patch, a piece of gum, that sort of thing. Worrying is no different. You can't just turn off your worrying like you turn off a faucet. You need to substitute something else. The Expert says that you need to substitute prayer. When you get an urge to worry, pray. When you think you need to worry, pray. Take the monkey off your back in every detail of your life and give it to God through prayer.

He will be gracious if you ask for help.
He will respond instantly to the sound of your cries.
ISAIAH 30:19

SPIRITUAL GROWTH

Consider your spiritual growth as a process instead of an event.

Spiritual growth doesn't happen all at once. It is a lifetime process. The reasons should be obvious. First of all, we continue to live in a sinful world (and in sinful bodies) so we'll never be perfect in our lifetime. But we can make progress, and as we do so, we'll be sinning less and less. Secondly, we continually find ourselves in new situations. If it seems that they become increasingly more difficult, that's probably true. God uses them to strengthen your faith. Thirdly, we gain a greater understanding about God as we learn to depend upon Him. Finally, spiritual growth doesn't happen all at once because there is so much to learn about God. Even in an entire lifetime we cannot learn all of the mysteries about Him.

The more you grow like this,
the more you will become productive and useful in
your knowledge of our Lord Jesus Christ.
2 PETER 1:8

COMFORT OTHERS

*One of the reasons God comforts us is so that
we can comfort others.*

There are certain things God gives us that we couldn't possibly give to others. For example, God saves us by His grace, but there's no way we can save anyone else. Nor can we heal others, give others a future and a hope, or forgive sins. We accept those things and thank God for them knowing they can't be duplicated.

There are other things God gives us that He expects us to give to others. Forgiveness is one of those things. God expects us to forgive others just as He has forgiven us (Matt. 6:14). God loves us, and He expects us to love others (1 John 4:11). God also comforts us, and He expects us to comfort others. If God has given you a lot of comfort in your life, it means you have done a lot of suffering. Now use your experiences to help relieve the suffering of others.

---

*I would speak in a way that helps you.
I would try to take away your grief.*
JOB 16:5

PREPARE NOW FOR ETERNITY

You are investing in eternity when you spend time with God.

Were you one of those kids who procrastinated in school? There are one or two in every classroom. They don't start the science project until the night before it's due. They don't read the book until the day before the oral report. And they don't study for the exam until the last minute. During the time they should be working, they are goofing off. The moment of truth comes when the comment on the report card reads: "Does not make good use of time."

That would be a terrible comment for God to say about us. He has given us a limited amount of time to work for His Kingdom. We have exactly until we die or until Christ returns. Since we don't know when either of those will happen, we shouldn't procrastinate. Make good use of the time God has given to you.

------

*Make the most of every opportunity
for doing good in these evil days.*
EPHESIANS 5:16

GOD IN YOU

People are attracted to enthusiasm.

There are two kinds of enthusiastic people. The first kind gets on your nerves. This is the old school motivational speaker whose enthusiasm is generated night after night in a memorized speech. He might appear enthusiastic on the outside, but inside he's just going through the motions.

The other kind of enthusiasm is genuine. It comes from inside and reflects a love for life and a love for people.

Christians should be the most enthusiastic people of all, because they have God in their lives. If you have doubts about this, just look at the word *enthusiasm*. It comes from two Greek words: *en*, meaning *in;* and *theos*, which is the word for *God*. In other words, enthusiasm means *God in you*. When God is in your life and you know He is working in everything you do, you can't help but be enthusiastic.

It was your enthusiasm that stirred up
many of them to begin helping.
2 CORINTHIANS 9:2

Talk about Others

People who talk a lot about themselves seldom want to hear what others have to say.

They say the sweetest sound we hear is the sound of our own voice, not because we like how our voice sounds, but because we like to hear ourselves talk. If we didn't, why would we talk so much?

You already know all about yourself, so why would you want to talk about yourself, except to impress others? What you don't realize is that the only thing you impress them with is your pride.

When you talk to others, talk *about* others (and we're not talking gossip here). Ask them questions. Find out what they think and what makes them tick. Don't worry about stating your opinion. When you show interest in others, others find you interesting, and it's only a matter of time before they want to know what makes you tick.

"For the proud will be humbled,
but the humble will be honored."
Luke 18:14

THANKING GOD

Thank the Lord each day for His gifts to you.

We too often take for granted the fact that God is always with us. His protection is constant; His comfort is ever-present. Wouldn't it be tragic if God remembered to attend to us only as often as we remembered to be thankful to Him.

Make it a regular part of your life to thank the Lord for His continuing mercies. Mealtime is a great way to remember. Saying a prayer over your food isn't really required. (It doesn't sterilize the food or give it a nutritional boost.) But since you remember to eat several times a day, take that opportunity to spend a minute or two acknowledging God's importance in your life.

God wouldn't let a moment go by without thinking of you. Try not to let a meal go by without thinking of Him.

"When you go through deep waters and great trouble,
I will be with you. . . .
When you walk through the fire of oppression,
you will not be burned up; the flames will not consume you.
For I am the LORD, your God,
the Holy One of Israel, your Savior."
ISAIAH 43:2–3

MAKE SOMEONE HAPPY

*Personal happiness is most easily gained by
bringing happiness to others.*

Happiness may be temporary, but we all want it, and that's okay, as long as we don't depend on the emotion of happiness like an extreme athlete depends on adrenaline.

Here's another thing we need to realize about happiness: It's harder to come by when we place it in *things*. Whether we depend on cars, a home, a raise, an outfit, or a meal for happiness, our happiness meter is going to jump all over the place as these things come and go.

A better way to gain happiness is to do things for others. Make others happy, and the happiest person will be you. Make others happy all the time, and your happiness will turn to joy.

---

*For I hope to visit you soon and to talk with you face to face.
Then our joy will be complete.*
2 JOHN 12

GLORIFY GOD

*Glory is something you give,
not take, and the One Who deserves it the most is God.*

Why did God create us in the first place? Was it to populate and manage the earth God made? Did God create us so we could interact with each other and show love for one another? How about witnessing? Maybe God put us on this earth so we could tell others about Him? All of those are excellent reasons, but there's an even bigger reason why we're here. God wants us to glorify Him.

The meaning of glory is *gift*, literally a gift of honor and praise. In everything we do, God wants us to glorify Him. According to the *Westminster Confession of Faith*, our "chief and highest end is to glorify God, and to fully enjoy Him forever." That's what happens when you honor God and give Him the praise. You enjoy Him forever.

---

*Whatever you eat or drink or whatever you do,
you must do all for the glory of God.*
1 CORINTHIANS 10:31

LOYALTY

Be as loyal to your friends as you want them to be to you.

There is a big difference between acquaintances and friends. Acquaintances are people that you know. They pop into your life (whether you want them to or not) as the result of your circumstances. So, you have acquaintances at work, in your neighborhood, and at church. These are people who may be very nice, but your relationship with them is defined more by contact than by commitment.

One of the characteristics that distinguishes acquaintances from friendship is loyalty. Friends are committed to each other. They are willing to make personal sacrifices for each other. They don't keep score of who owes a favor to whom. If you have true friends, then thank God for them. They are rare commodities. If you need to increase your friendship network and find a few, then start by being the kind of friend you would want to have.

---

*"The greatest love is shown when
people lay down their lives for their friends."*
JOHN 15:13

LEADERSHIP

*One of the sobering characteristics of leadership is
that God expects more of leaders than followers.*

Leaders like to think they are a tough breed. Every once in a while you'll see a sign like this on a leader's desk: *Lead, follow, or get out of the way.*

There's no question that it takes a special person with unique qualities to be a leader, but here's a fact that should make every leader—especially leaders who are Christians—sit up and take notice. God notices leaders, God watches leaders, and God expects a lot out of leaders.

The reason, we suspect, is that leaders are more responsible for others than followers are. A teacher is responsible to God for his students, a CEO is responsible for her employees, a pastor is responsible for his congregation, and parents are responsible for their children. We're not saying that followers don't have responsibilities, too, but leaders have a greater responsibility to demonstrate wisdom, respect, and integrity.

---

*"Much is required from those to whom much is given,
and much more is required from those to whom
much more is given."*
LUKE 12:48

THE BEST SUCCESS FORMULA

Rather than trying to make a success of yourself,
ask God to do the job.

Throughout history the "formula for success" has changed according to the times. An older formula would be something like "Put your nose to the grindstone." Since we don't use grindstones anymore (and we certainly wouldn't want to stick our noses on one), we've come up with more current formulas, such as "Change or die."

Here is a success formula as timeless as God Himself (which stands to reason, since God came up with it): "Repent and be saved." Now, we admit that you are more likely to see this formula on a street preacher's sign than the cover of a self-help book. It doesn't exactly inspire you to go out there and make something of yourself.

But God doesn't want you to go out there and make a success of yourself, at least not in the spiritual sense. What He wants you to do is ask Him to make you successful.

Beg the LORD to save you—all you who are humble,
all you who uphold justice.
Walk humbly and do what is right.
ZEPHANIAH 2:3

What Happens in You

*What happens in you is more important than
what happens to you.*

We give a lot of attention to the changing events of our lives. We are constantly thinking about the next job, an upcoming vacation, or going to that new restaurant. You might even have one of those calendars the size of a billboard stuck to your refrigerator to keep track of family activities. Monitoring changes in your schedule is important, but it is not as important as monitoring the changes in your heart.

Don't forget that changes should be happening inside of you as well. We are not talking about gastrointestinal activities; we're referring to the strengthening of your character as you grow closer to God. Are you monitoring your progress? Do you notice that your thoughts and actions are becoming more like what God wants them to be?

Spend as much time today thinking about your character as you spend planning your calendar.

---

*The LORD has already told you what is good,
and this is what he requires: to do what is right,
to love mercy, and to walk humbly with your God.*
MICAH 6:8

YOU AREN'T LUCKY

*You may not understand everything that happens to you,
but you can be sure everything good comes from God.*

We are quick to blame God for the bad stuff that happens to us ("God, where were you when Grandpa got cancer?") as well as to our world ("That hurricane was an act of God"). On the other hand, when something good happens, we often say, "Well, that was lucky."

We must understand that nothing in our lives and in our world happens outside of God's knowledge and control. Even though we don't understand why God allows certain things to occur, we must never accept the notion that God is powerless. He loves us completely and would never do anything to harm us. But until Christ returns to "make things new" (Rev. 21:5), the world and its inhabitants will groan under the burden of sin (Rom. 8:22).

Anything good that happens to you is not because you are lucky or fortunate. Luck is powerless to do anything. God is the One Who gives you all good things.

---

*Whatever is good and perfect comes to us from God above,
who created all heaven's lights.*
JAMES 1:17

Rely on God's Perspective

Sometimes you have to believe it before you can see it.

Since God is sovereign and in control of all things, it's difficult to understand why He allows some things to happen to us. We aren't puzzled by "Why does God let bad things happen to good people?" because many of the "good" people don't believe in Him. We are perplexed by the question of "Why does He let bad things happen to those of us who love Him?"

Perhaps no one has the complete answer. We may have to wait until heaven for that. In the meantime, let's remind ourselves that God's personality traits include love and omniscience. He cannot do anything that is not in the best interests of His children. And He knows everything, so He has the long-term perspective on what we need now to prepare us for the future.

We may not understand it, but we can trust that He knows what He is doing.

And we know that God causes everything to
work together for the good of those who love God
and are called according to his purpose for them.
ROMANS 8:28

SEASONS OF LIFE

Variety may be the spice of life, but God provides the seasons.

Just as there are seasons in nature, there are seasons in life. As you progress in your spiritual life, you will go through seasons of change and growth as well as dormancy and doubt.

Spring is the season of joy, when new growth occurs. God seems very close in both the big and small stuff during this season of life.

Summer is made for relaxing, vacationing, and renewing. This is when your life seems like it's in cruise control with no concerns.

Fall can lull you into complacency. You may even take God for granted. Fall is the season of disappointments and unfulfilled expectations.

Winter is the time when you need God more than ever, even though He seems far away. Call out to God and He will answer—not by removing your winter—but by giving you the strength to get through it.

There is a time for everything,
a season for every activity under heaven.
ECCLESIASTES 3:1

WHAT KIND OF WORKER ARE YOU?

You will find more significance in the quality of the work you accomplish than in the quantity of the work you attempt.

We refuse to put a "Christian bumper sticker" on our cars. We aren't ashamed to declare our love for the Lord, but we don't want anyone to think less of God (or Christians) if they consider our driving habits to be less than exemplary. It all has to do with projecting the image that God deserves—excellence in everything.

If you belong to God, and if other people know it, they will be evaluating God by what they see in you. This means that we need to work diligently and excellently at our assigned tasks. Few things leave a worse impression than a job left unfinished or a job poorly done.

God intends for us to do good things at our jobs, in our communities, and for our families. But for these things to be truly good, they must be done well.

For we are God's masterpiece.
He has created us anew in Christ Jesus,
so that we can do the good things he planned for us long ago.
EPHESIANS 2:10

THE HEART TELLS ALL

*The measure of your success is not what is in your wallet,
but what is in your heart.*

In a culture obsessed with money and possessions, God's people need to constantly evaluate their definition of success. It's not that the definition should change, mind you. We just need to make sure we aren't following the culture by making our stuff the measure of our success.

You don't have to tell someone, "It's money that matters to me," or "Money isn't the measure of my success," for them to know where you stand. Where you give your time and what you do with your money will speak for you more than your words.

Your heart will follow whatever is most important to you. If it's money, that's where your heart will be. If it's putting God and others first, then your heart will show it. By heart we mean passion, emotion, priorities, and character. The heart tells all.

---

*Those who love money will never have enough.
How absurd to think that wealth brings true happiness!*
ECCLESIASTES 5:10

Have a Good Heart

*Unlike a tree, you have the ability to choose
the fruit your life produces.*

Jesus said that you can tell what is in a person's heart by listening to what that person says. He used the word "heart" to mean a person's true character and feelings. If someone frequently gossips, lies, and speaks negatively about others, you have a pretty good impression of his character. Likewise, you can easily guess the character of a person whose words are encouraging, kind, and truthful.

People can't see your heart, but they can see (and hear) what your heart produces. It's like the fruit on a tree. You know what kind of tree you're looking at by the fruit it produces. Jesus said, "Make a tree good, and its fruit will be good. Make a tree bad, and its fruit will be bad" (Matt. 12:33). Make it your goal to produce good fruit by the power of the Holy Spirit.

---

*"A good person produces good words from a good heart,
and an evil person produces evil words from an evil heart."*
MATTHEW 12:35

A TEACHABLE SPIRIT

You'll never be a "know-it-all"
if you try to be more teachable each day.

Your education doesn't stop when you receive a diploma. Even if you complete your formal schooling, plan to keep learning. And if you never received a diploma, don't worry—the bulk of what you need to learn for the rest of your life wasn't taught in a classroom anyway.

Your "lifetime learning" will come from many sources. First, God has plenty to teach you. We predict you'll enjoy reaching deeper levels of understanding as you learn from and about Him. Secondly, you can learn a lot about yourself from your friends (if you are perceptive and receptive to their criticism). And you can learn from young children (your own or others) because their childish responses are similar to how we often behave with God.

There is a lot left to learn if you are willing to be teachable.

Let those who are wise understand these things.
Let those who are discerning listen carefully.
The paths of the LORD are true and right,
and righteous people live by walking in them.
HOSEA 14:9

TWO NATURES—TWO RESULTS

God will never put you into a position where
you don't have a choice.

As a Christian, you can choose to live on your own power, which the Bible calls "the old sinful nature." If that's your choice, here are the results of your power: "sexual immorality, impure thoughts, eagerness for lustful pleasure, idolatry, participation in demonic activities, hostility, quarreling, jealousy, outbursts of anger, selfish ambition, divisions. . .envy, drunkenness, wild parties, and other kinds of sin" (Gal. 5:19–21). Not a pretty picture.

Or you can choose to live "according to your new life in the Holy Spirit" (Gal. 5:16). If that's your choice, here are the results of the Spirit's power in your life: love, joy, peace, patience, kindness, goodness, faithfulness, gentleness, and self-control" (Gal. 5:22–23). It's not up to us to produce "this kind of fruit." We just have to give control to the Holy Spirit, Who does the producing.

So I advise you to live according to
your new life in the Holy Spirit.
Then you won't be doing what your sinful nature craves.
GALATIANS 5:16

A FAMILY RESEMBLANCE

Be a person whose life is marked by truth, integrity, and passion.

Many people share a family resemblance with their parents. It might be curly hair, or a toothy grin. Maybe it is the way you walk or a distinctive laugh. When people see a resemblance of this type, they know what family you belong to.

If you want people to know that you belong to God, your "family resemblance" should be godliness. That trait might look like this in your life:

- *Knowing the truth*—which comes from studying God's Word;
- *Acting with integrity*—which comes from doing God's Word; and
- *Living with passion*—which comes from sharing God's Word.

If you have these characteristics in your life, people will easily see the family resemblance between you and your heavenly Father.

But all will be well for those who are godly.
Tell them, "You will receive a wonderful reward!"
ISAIAH 3:10

DON'T TAKE PITY

Help the helpless and give to the needy,
but do it out of compassion, not pity.

It's easy to take pity on others, but we should never offer our help out of pity. Pity demeans others. You feel sorry for them, but you keep them at arm's length. You are grateful that you aren't in their position, so you make a donation and change the channel, thankful that you're not like them. That kind of giving is hollow and hypocritical.

By contrast, compassion gets you involved emotionally as well as financially. You really *feel* for the person in need. Your heart "goes out" to the people who are helpless, so you respond generously, knowing that your money is useful, but hardly a substitute for the real work you must do (for a look at the real work, see tomorrow's devotional).

When you are compassionate, your giving comes from your heart *and* your wallet, and one is never a substitute for the other.

You are generous because of your faith.
PHILEMON 6

BE WISE IN YOUR COMPASSION

True generosity involves your head as well as your heart.

When it comes to generosity, there are two questions to ask. First, does it come from your heart? The Bible says that God loves a cheerful giver (2 Cor. 9:7). If your motive isn't right—let's say you're trying to get recognition or you want some favor from someone in exchange for your generosity—then it doesn't matter how much you give away. You aren't being generous. Before you give anything away, examine your own motives.

The second question to ask is this: Is your generosity productive? As a Christian, you are called to a higher standard so that your giving can make a difference in the lives of people in need. Don't just write checks and hope the organizations use your money wisely. Hold them and yourself accountable by getting involved, thereby multiplying your investment in God's work.

And I am praying that
you will really put your generosity to work,
for in so doing you will come to an understanding
of all the good things we can do for Christ.
PHILEMON 6

TRUE CHARITY

*True charity doesn't worry about whether
the contribution is tax deductible.*

Keep track of the money that you give to your church, ministries, and charities. These contributions are usually tax deductible; you're being a good steward of the Lord's money if you take advantage of legitimate income tax deductions. But your decision about giving your money shouldn't be determined solely by whether the donation is deductible.

Let God direct your charitable decisions. You need to rely on His guidance for when, how much, and to whom your gifts should be made. Sometimes you'll need to give when there is no tax deduction available (such as paying the car repair bill for a friend who has been laid off work). Other times, you may need to give cash anonymously.

Look for ways you can use your money to help others (whether it is deductible or not).

---

*You must each make up your own mind
as to how much you should give.
Don't give reluctantly or in response to pressure.
For God loves the person who gives cheerfully.*
2 CORINTHIANS 9:7

ALWAYS ENOUGH

The generous person always has more than enough;
the greedy person never has enough.

The principle of generosity is verifiable in Scripture. We aren't going to go as far as some people and tell you, "The more you give, the more you get." That idea seems to be based on the false principle that the motive for giving money away is getting rich yourself. In our view, a better principle is illustrated by the prophet Elijah and the widow. Elijah depended on the generosity of others for just about every material need (most prophets lived this way), but when God sent him to a poor widow, he had to wonder (and so did she). Yet an amazing thing happened. As the widow gave Elijah what little food she had, there was always enough food left over for her and her son.

That's the way it is with generous people. They don't get rich because of their generosity, but they always seem to have enough.

For no matter how much they used,
there was always enough left in the containers,
just as the LORD had promised. . .
1 KINGS 17:16

THE TWO SIDES OF GOSSIP

Listening to gossip is as bad as spreading it.

There are three types of people who are unfairly held in low regard in our society: used car salesmen, lawyers, and gossips. For the most part, used car salesmen are a good bunch; it's too bad that their reputation is tarnished by a few bad ones. Lawyers aren't all bad, either, but we have to ridicule them because the lawyer jokes are so funny (and so well-deserved). And the gossips are only half as bad as we think they are.

Don't misunderstand. Gossip is bad—always and totally. But the people who do it—the *gossips*—are only half of the problem. The other half of the blame must be laid on the people who *listen* to the gossip. If everyone refused to listen to gossip, the problem would be solved.

Since your ears can't close by themselves, using your feet can help. Just walk away whenever you overhear gossip.

A troublemaker plants seeds of strife;
gossip separates the best of friends.
PROVERBS 16:28

GIVE GLORY TO GOD

It's human nature to take credit. It's God's nature to receive glory.

There's a difference between doing things for God in order to impress others and doing things for God in order to impress, well, God! When your motive is to impress others, your good deeds—the ones God wants you to do—are going to bring attention to you. People will praise *you* for your generosity and your efforts.

When your motive is to impress and please God, that changes everything. You are still out there, enthusiastically serving others, giving your time, talents, and resources, but you let the spotlight fall on God. He gets the glory, not you.

That's the way God wants us to work. We shouldn't stay so much in the background that nobody knows why we're doing something, but neither should we be out in front hogging the light. God wants us to shine the light on Him so everyone can see.

"Let your good deeds shine out for all to see,
so that everyone will praise your heavenly Father."
MATTHEW 5:16

An Affordable Lifestyle

*You aren't living within your means if
you have to borrow money to do it.*

There are two problems with borrowing money; one is obvious and the other is a bit more subtle. The obvious drawback to borrowing money is the fact that you have to pay it back. Repayment never seems like a problem when the loan is made, but that's only because the repayment schedule hasn't started yet. When the due date approaches, the stress increases.

The subtle problem with borrowing is that it distracts you from focusing on God. Debt demands your attention. You are either scurrying to pay your creditors, or you are busy hiding from them. You'll find few spare moments to be meditating on God if you're constantly worried about the next monthly payment. It is difficult to see God when you are buried in debt.

Avoid getting into excessive debt. Better yet, avoid borrowing whenever possible. Adjust your lifestyle so you can manage with the money you have.

---

*Just as the rich rule the poor,
so the borrower is servant to the lender.*
PROVERBS 22:7

A NEW HEART

Contrary to popular belief,
the hardest part of the human body is not the head,
but the heart.

What is a hardened heart? In the mildest sense, a hardened heart is a stubborn heart. It can also be a heart turned against God. This was the case of Pharaoh, who refused to let God's people go (Exod. 7:13).

What about today? Are there people whose hearts are hardened against God? Absolutely. It's not for us to point fingers and try to identify those we think are guilty, because in a very real sense, all of us start out with a hardened heart. Every one of us is turned against God, and we remain that way until we turn our hearts over to God. When that happens, God promises to replace our hard hearts with hearts that follow after Him. Not only that, but God also gives us the Holy Spirit, so our hearts will never harden again.

"And I will give you a new heart with new and right desires,
and I will put a new spirit in you. . . .
And I will put my Spirit in you so you will obey my laws
and do whatever I command."
EZEKIEL 36:26–27

PRAISE

You can't praise God too much.

Did you know that God loves to be praised? Maybe you have mistakenly assumed that He doesn't need to hear us give Him the credit for the wonderful things that happen in our lives. After all, He is the biggest, most powerful being in the universe. Why would He care what we measly humans have to say?

Well, here are two reasons why we need to praise God. First of all, He should be honored. He is so magnificent that He deserves it. Second of all, we need to thank Him constantly because it reminds us that what we have comes from Him.

Make sure that your prayers aren't all about what you want God to give you. Spend time praising Him for Who He is and what He has already done for you.

All honor to the God and Father of our Lord Jesus Christ,
for it is by his boundless mercy that God has given us
the privilege of being born again.
1 PETER 1:3

STAY STRONG AND SWIFT

Take Satan seriously but never fear him.

Few people take Satan seriously, because he's the funny guy in the red suit with the horns and a pitchfork, cracking jokes and overacting. Or he's the sinister bad guy, kind of scary but not so tough that a single Hollywood superhero can't defeat him in the course of a movie.

What if Satan's image was more like a lion? Not so bad, you say? Consider this. On the outside, Satan is an impressive-looking creature, able to disguise himself as some kind of king. In reality, he's an opportunist, and a sadistic one at that. Just like the lion, Satan's main objective is to attack the weak and the stragglers in the herd. You'll never see the king of the jungle go after the strong and the swift, and neither will Satan. He preys on the weak and the slow. To keep Satan off your back, stay strong and swift in the Lord.

Be careful! Watch out for attacks from the Devil,
your great enemy.
He prowls around like a roaring lion,
looking for some victim to devour.
1 PETER 5:8

STICK WITH IT

To win the race you need a goal.
To win the human race you need Jesus.

Everything that's worthwhile in life requires perseverance. Why? Because worthwhile projects and worthwhile goals are never easy. That's especially true of living as a Christ-follower. There's nothing more worthwhile, but sometimes there's nothing more difficult. Everything in this world seems to run contrary to how you are called to live. Yet even as you persevere, you must realize that you can't run and finish this marathon race called the Christian life alone. You need Jesus, Who not only saved you, but Who also helps you right now in your struggle against discouragement and sin. Do you want to live your life like a champion? Do you want to win the race? Keep your eyes on Jesus. Your faith depends on it.

And let us run with endurance the race that
God has set before us.
We do this by keeping our eyes on Jesus,
on whom our faith depends from start to finish.
HEBREWS 12:1–2

RIGHTS VS. RESPONSIBILITIES

You are responsible to God to become
what God has made it possible for you to become.

Political groups and social organizations are always talking about the "rights" of their members. They want the full entitlement to the benefits that are rightfully theirs. Rights are all about "me, me, me."

That is not the attitude God wants you to have. He wants you to forget about your rights and focus on your responsibilities. He wants you fully engaged in helping others. Responsibilities are all about "you, you, you."

God wouldn't be a very popular politician in our society. Most people want to be served and enjoy their privileges. God calls us to be submissive and put the interests of others above our own. It is possible only if God can change your attitude. Are you willing to let Him?

Your attitude should be the same that Christ Jesus had.
Though he was God, he did not demand
and cling to his rights as God. He made himself nothing;
he took the humble position of a slave
and appeared in human form.
PHILIPPIANS 2:5–7

A GRATEFUL HEART

You can't always control the kind of service you receive,
but you can always control the kind of gratitude you deliver.

Service is big these days. A lot of companies have built their reputations on service, so we have come to expect it. But what if the package you were expecting doesn't arrive the next day? What if the restaurant server messes up your order? What if the minimum wage retail clerk talks on the phone rather than waiting on you?

Are you going to yell at someone over the phone? Are you going to refuse to leave your server a tip? Are you going to ask to speak to the manager so you can really chew him out? Sometimes it is necessary to correct a wrong, but most of our ranting over poor service is totally unnecessary and uncalled for. Regardless of the kind of service we receive, we need to always deliver the heart of gratitude and grace that God shows to us.

No matter what happens, always be thankful,
for this is God's will for you who belong to Christ Jesus.
1 THESSALONIANS 5:18

A GENEROUS HEART

Feeling good about yourself begins with serving others.

In this age when some people have a net worth equal to the gross national product of small nations, how do you know when *you* have enough? And do you have enough to feel good about your situation?

If you think that having a certain amount of money will make you feel secure, think again. That will never happen. Whether you have a zero balance in your bank account or enough to retire on, you are never going to feel like you have enough—if your contentment is tied to your net worth.

The only way to reach that point of personal satisfaction is to have a generous heart, no matter how much or how little you have. If you cling to your possessions, they will never satisfy you. If you hold them loosely and share with others, you will always have enough.

Give generously to those in need,
always being ready to share with others.
1 TIMOTHY 6:18

CONFRONTATION

Your best friends will be the ones who bring out the best in you.

Friends are quick to compliment each other, but confrontation comes much harder. In fact, many people will choose to avoid confronting a friend with an important issue. (But if you dodge what needs to be done, then you aren't much of a friend after all.) Although it may be difficult, at times you may have to oppose a friend who is doing something that is clearly wrong.

Do you have a Christian friend whose behavior blatantly defies what Jesus taught? Are you avoiding a confrontation with this friend? If so, pray about how to approach this subject with your friend. Remember to do it in love.

Read 1 Corinthians 13 for a little guidance.

But when Peter came to Antioch,
I had to oppose him publicly,
speaking strongly against what he was doing,
for it was very wrong.
GALATIANS 2:11

GOD WILL BE WITH YOU

God doesn't promise you a life without difficulties.
But He does promise that He will always be with you.

Don't let anybody tell you that a life with God is a life without troubles. Far from it. Sometimes it seems that your troubles begin the moment you trust God. Yet we continue to "sell" Christianity as a sort of Pollyanna religion that offers happiness to all who sign up.

There's nothing in the Bible about that, so you've got to figure it isn't true. What the Bible does say is that troubles will come your way, and when they do, you need to use them as a way to grow closer to God. When God helps you through your problems, whether big or small, your joy increases in proportion to your faith. You know you can count on God whenever troubles come your way.

For when your faith is tested,
your endurance has a chance to grow.
JAMES 1:3

DISCOURAGEMENT

If you are feeling down, it's because you aren't looking up.

A good way to avoid discouragement is to correct your vision. If your difficulties are discouraging you, then you are spending too much time looking at your situation and not enough time looking at God. When you are discouraged:

Look at how God has been faithful to you in the past. Remember how He faithfully protected you and met your needs.

Let God work in your life right now. Rely on Him for your strength and hope. Your reliance on God in your tough times can be an example to others.

Look ahead to when you will spend eternity in the presence of God in heaven. Your current troubles won't last long compared to the joy that will last forever.

We are pressed on every side by troubles,
but we are not crushed and broken.
We are perplexed, but we don't give up and quit.
So we don't look at the troubles we can see right now;
rather, we look forward to what we have not yet seen.
For the troubles we see will soon be over,
but the joys to come will last forever.
2 CORINTHIANS 4:8, 18

THE ESSENCE OF LOYALTY

Be loyal to people; more importantly, be loyal to God.

Not all virtues require the same amount of effort. For example, patience takes a lot of work because we have to do something that goes against our natural impulsiveness. The same goes for purity. By contrast, the virtue of loyalty requires little effort, because it's the natural extension of love.

Just telling someone, "I'm going to be loyal to you," doesn't prove your loyalty any more than telling someone, "I love you," proves your love. When you announce your intentions and then follow through on your promises, you're showing loyalty. When you defend the one you love from accusations and misunderstandings, you're being loyal.

It's easy to be loyal to someone you love, but are you loyal to God? You've told God what you're going to do, but have you followed through on your promises? You know what God has done for you, but have you defended Him when others accuse Him?

"I will go wherever you go and live wherever you live. Your people will be my people, and your God will be my God."
RUTH 1:16

TAKE YOUR PLACE

No one is too good to stay out of church,
and no one is too bad to go in.

Is there a place for you in God's family? You better believe it! Never think that you are an unimportant part of God's plan. He has specifically and uniquely equipped you, and your abilities are needed and useful to other Christians.

God uses an analogy of a human body to describe how all Christians function together. Just as every part of the human body plays a vital role in life, every Christian plays a vital role in the ministry of the church.

God wants you to find your place in ministry. You won't be fulfilling God's plan for you if you don't. And your church will be incomplete without your involvement.

The human body has many parts,
but the many parts make up only one body.
So it is with the body of Christ.
This makes for harmony among the members,
so that all the members care for each other equally.
1 CORINTHIANS 12:12, 25

RISE ABOVE

When you're content to settle for something,
you end up being average.

To say that Jesus doesn't like mediocrity is an understatement. Jesus said, "I know all the things you do, that you are neither hot nor cold. I wish you were one or the other! But since you are like lukewarm water, I will spit you out of my mouth!" (Rev. 3:15–16). Why does Jesus react so strongly? Because when we're mediocre, we're neither good nor bad. To be mediocre is to go halfway. It's being average when you have the potential to be great. Ask any coach or parent. There's nothing more frustrating than watching someone with potential do nothing.

Jesus offers a life beyond anything we can imagine, yet often we hang on to our mediocre existence like a beggar grasping a loaf of bread when a feast awaits. Jesus won't force Himself on you, but He wants you to turn from your indifference, rise above your mediocrity, and be sold out to Him.

"I advise you to buy gold from me—
gold that has been purified by fire.
Then you will be rich."
REVELATION 3:18

NOT A RELIGION

Religions are man's attempt to find God,
but Christ was God's method to reach mankind.

Many people mistakenly believe that Christianity is a religion with a long list of "do's and don'ts" (mostly don'ts). Such an opinion is wrong on two counts. First of all, Christianity is not a religion; that connotes a highly structured organization and hierarchy. At its heart, Christianity is just a relationship (between you and God with Christ providing the connection). Secondly, there are no "rules" that you are required to follow to earn God's love, and there is no list of "don'ts" that would disqualify you from it.

Don't let the "no rules" throw you. Certain behavior is wrong (lying, stealing, and immorality). And some types of behavior, while not wrong in themselves, can become inappropriate if not handled in moderation (working, eating, and golf).

Some people are lost without boundaries, so you may find this question helpful: "Do you believe God is pleased with what you are doing?"

Don't act thoughtlessly,
but try to understand what the Lord wants you to do.
EPHESIANS 5:17

THE CHURCH BODY NEEDS YOU

Discover your spiritual gift.
Then, get involved in a ministry so you can use it.

The great thing about spiritual gifts is that everybody has at least one. Some people have more than one, but you have at least one special spiritual ability given to you by the Holy Spirit. The purpose of spiritual gifts is simple: "A spiritual gift is given to each of us as a means of helping the entire church" (1 Cor. 12:7).

The apostle Paul compares the church to a human body, which needs all of its parts to function (1 Cor. 12:12). We may think certain body parts are more important than others, but you'll never hear your eye tell your big toe, "Hey, smelly, I'm better than you." Your body needs every part to function effectively, and so does the church.

Next time you think the church doesn't need you, remember that you have a gift to give. Search the Scriptures, pray, and ask your pastor to help you discover your spiritual gift.

Now there are different kinds of spiritual gifts,
but it is the same Holy Spirit who is the source of them all.
1 CORINTHIANS 12:4

FRACTURED FAMILIES

All families spend time together,
but the best families don't need a television set to do it.

Our culture's concept of "family" is fractured. Husbands and wives battle in divorce courts. Children sue parents over custody. The government attempts to legislate relationships.

God knows about the family. After all, He invented it. God designed and intends the family to reflect His love. This attitude of love should exist between the husband and wife, and between the parents and children. Every family member should respond to the others with kindness, as if they were responding to God Himself.

Your family may be fractured. It may not be all that you want it to be. You can begin a restoration process in your family by showing God's love. Whether you are a spouse, or a parent or a child, be God's ambassador in your family.

So again I say, each man must love his wife as he loves himself,
and the wife must respect her husband.
Children, obey your parents because you belong to the Lord,
for this is the right thing to do.
EPHESIANS 5:33–6:1

CRITICISM TAKES NO EFFORT

Criticism and finding fault are not spiritual gifts.

Spiritual gifts are designed by God to help the church. Criticism and finding fault are not helpful. Therefore, criticism and finding fault are not spiritual gifts.

This little bit of logic was brought to you by the apostle Paul, whom God inspired to say, "You should desire the most helpful gifts" (1 Cor. 12:31).

But do we listen to Paul? No, we have a better idea.

Why aspire to help, heal, teach, encourage, or serve others—when we can more easily criticize and find fault in others? Maybe because criticism comes more naturally for us. It's what we do when we live by our old sin nature—which takes no effort at all—rather than live by the power of the Holy Spirit—which requires a daily, willful surrender to God.

But if instead of showing love among yourselves
you are always biting and devouring one another, watch out!
Beware of destroying one another.
GALATIANS 5:15

SYMPATHY

*Sometimes the most effective words of comfort
are no words at all.*

Tragedy in a friend's life can leave you speechless—
not because you are shocked, but because you don't know what
to say. You might be very concerned and sympathetic, but you
avoid talking with your friend because you can't think of an
appropriate thing to say. So you say nothing.

We are all in that position from time to time, so don't
feel too bad about it. But don't let your momentary muteness
prevent you from being a comfort to your friends. Is it possible to offer sympathy without saying anything? Sure. In fact,
your friend may not feel like engaging in a gabfest anyway. It
may be enough for you to extend a hug or spend a while sitting in silence with your friend.

A lot can be said between friends when you don't say
anything.

"Comfort, comfort my people," says your God.
ISAIAH 40:1

SEEKING GOD TAKES WORK

God will never send a thirsty soul to a dry well.

Nothing worth seeking is easy to find. Columbus didn't just get into a boat, sail for a couple of days, and find the New World. We didn't put a man on the moon because a bunch of scientists and astronauts had a free weekend and thought, *Hey, we've got nothing better to do. Let's launch a spaceship.* Great discoveries take place after great effort and persistence.

We understand that, so why do we expend such little effort when we look for God? Why don't we persist when we ask Him for our needs and the needs of others? So many people look for God with a minimum of effort and then give up. They even conclude that God isn't there. Seeking and knowing God takes effort, time, and persistence. It also takes faith. If you seek God, you must believe that He will answer.

Anyone who wants to come to him
must believe that there is a God
and that he rewards those who sincerely seek him.
HEBREWS 11:6

GOD'S FAITHFULNESS

Looking back on what God has done for you in the past should strengthen your faith for the future.

Fans of professional sports teams are usually fanatics for statistics. They know how each member of the team has performed in the past season. They can tell you a pitcher's strikeout average per game, or a quarterback's third down conversion percentage. Actually, the statistics have more than historical value; they can give you an *indication* of how the player will perform in a future situation. But there is no guarantee that the player will match his or her past performance.

We can think of only one example where the past record is a guarantee of future performance: God. You can rely on His record of past performance for the future. Throughout your entire life, He has been there for you. That won't change. He is the same yesterday, today, and forever.

You don't have to fear the future because you know what God has done in the past.

For God has said, "I will never fail you.
I will never forsake you."
HEBREWS 13:5

TEAMWORK

Commit yourself to projects; dedicate yourself to people.

There's nothing wrong with projects, but projects never accomplished anything. It's people that do the accomplishing, because people do the projects. Keep that in mind when you begin your next project. Your performance is important, and it's important that you commit yourself to giving your best effort. But the people you involve are even more important.

In today's project-driven culture, you are wise to bring other people—with their diverse talents and gifts—into your projects. It's called teamwork. Whether you work in a business, a factory, a classroom, or a church, you need to recognize that teams—where people with complementary skills and passions work together for the good of the organization—are a must.

This is no new concept. God has already said in His Word, "Now all of you together are Christ's body" (1 Cor. 12:27).

We belong to each other,
and each of us needs all the others.
ROMANS 12:5

WHO (OR WHAT) DO YOU LOVE?

*You can tell a lot about your priorities by
reviewing your checkbook ledger.*

If your house were on fire and you had time to re-trieve only one item, what would it be? Most likely, it would be the thing that has the most value to you. The value could be financial worth, or it may just be great sentimental value. Your answer—whether you chose the shoebox full of cash or the family photo album—will reveal what's important to you.

Many people proclaim to love God, but their actions don't support that proclamation. Their time, energy, and re-sources are devoted to other things. God isn't really important to them if they are able to ignore Him almost all of the time.

How about you? Are you in love with God? Don't answer this question verbally. Examine the actions and thoughts of your life. What do they reveal as being important to you?

---

*"Wherever your treasure is,
there your heart and thoughts will also be."*
MATTHEW 6:21

A Place for Tolerance

Know the difference between tolerance and permissiveness.

We make decisions about tolerance and permissiveness every day, and sometimes we confuse the two. When you are tolerant toward others, you are patient with them, even though their opinions or behavior may differ from yours. You may even be convinced the other person is dead wrong, but you can still tolerate him or her. Permission takes the person into account, but focuses more on the behavior. When you are permissive, you don't forbid the behavior of another.

So how do you distinguish between the two? Obviously, your permission counts only when you have authority over another person. You would never say, "I'm giving my boss permission to do such and such." Tolerance, on the other hand, respects and loves others while not necessarily endorsing their behavior. In fact, that characteristic is at the heart of tolerance, and this is what God asks you to do.

---

*Don't you realize how kind, tolerant, and patient
God is with you? Or don't you care?*
ROMANS 2:4

VALUING OTHERS

If you look for the best in people,
you are likely to find value in every person.

It seems that our natural tendency is to be critical of other people. (Maybe it makes us feel better about ourselves if we belittle someone else.) As with most of our natural tendencies and instincts, God wants us to act in the opposite manner.

Instead of finding faults at the outset, we should look for the good in every individual. Think of it as a type of treasure hunt. You're looking for the value in people. You may be surprised that you will find much more than you expected at the outset of your search.

We acknowledge that this may be particularly difficult to do with some individuals. But even with the most abrasive person, you won't come up empty in your treasure hunt. Every person has value because each of us is loved by God.

Now all of you together are Christ's body,
and each one of you is a separate and necessary part of it.
1 CORINTHIANS 12:27

LET THE CHILDREN COME

Teach children in some way throughout your life.

We must never forget that children are a gift from God. They are not our possessions, our property, or even our right. As Henri Nouwen wrote, "Our children are our most important guests."

We are responsible to care for and nurture our children, and we must also teach them. The greatest Teacher ever made it clear that we should never deny children who want us to bless and teach them. The disciples thought Jesus was too important and too busy to deal with children, but Jesus was quick to correct them. "Let the children come to me," He said.

No matter where you are in life, you need to be around children. Your own children are your first responsibility, but you should also invite the children of others to come to you. Give them your time, your teaching, and your love.

Then Jesus called for the children and said to the disciples,
"Let the children come to me. Don't stop them!
For the Kingdom of God belongs to such as these."
LUKE 18:16

ANGER

Keep your anger under control so it doesn't control you.

There are two kinds of anger. There is righteous anger that comes out of a godly response to sin. This is the kind of anger that God displays because sin is such an offense to Him. Jesus showed righteous anger when He chased the money changers out of the Temple (Matt. 21:12–13). Righteous anger is not a reaction to a personal offense, and God always controls it.

The second kind of anger is "personal anger." Losing your temper is personal anger. This is the type of anger that controls you. You say or do something you later regret. God is nowhere to be found in this type of anger. That's why the Bible warns against it.

Don't let your personal anger take control of your life.

Stop your anger! Turn from your rage!
PSALM 37:8

A TRUE FRIEND

A true friend can multiply your joy and divide your sorrow.

In your lifetime you will have thousands of acquaintances, hundreds of colleagues, and dozens of neighbors. But you will have only a few friends. That's not to say that you won't have lots of friendships. Some people make friends easily. You might be the kind of person who never met a stranger.

Don't confuse a casual friendship with a true friend. Even the friendliest person has only a few true friends, defined by honesty, loyalty, and sacrifice. A true friend possesses these qualities, whereas fair-weather friends disappear when you experience setbacks or don't give them what they need.

With that in mind, we're going to tell you the name of your best friend. You already know Him, and He just happens to be our best friend as well. His name is Jesus. He will never leave you, He will never forsake you, and He has already made the supreme sacrifice for you.

"I no longer call you servants,
because a master doesn't confide in his servants.
Now you are my friends,
since I have told you everything the Father told me."
JOHN 15:15

TIME FOR A HEART EXAM

*Hardness of the heart is more deadly than
hardening of the arteries.*

The devil made me do it." That isn't just a line made
famous by comedian Flip Wilson. It is also a popular excuse
that many people use when they are confronted with their
own sinful conduct. It makes for a good punch line, but it is a
lousy excuse.

The devil doesn't make you do anything. Your heart
does. (We aren't talking about the blood-pumping muscle in
your chest; we're referring to your inner spirit.) The heart of
every person is inclined toward sin from the moment of birth.
It doesn't get any better on its own. A heart transplant is
required if you are going to enjoy real life. Your sinful heart
must be replaced with a heart filled with God's love.

---

*"The human heart is most deceitful and desperately wicked.
Who really knows how bad it is?"*
JEREMIAH 17:9

SEEK WISDOM

If you seek wisdom over opportunity,
opportunity will usually follow.

No matter where you look, there's opportunity. It may not be knocking on your door, but all you have to do is drive around and you'll see opportunity calling out from billboards, bus stops, and anything else big enough for a sign. Watch television and you'll see more messages of opportunity. Surf the Internet and little banners will flash constantly: *Get rich quick! Save money now! Free Internet access!*

Your problem isn't opportunity. Opportunity is plentiful and cheap (and you usually get what you pay for). What you need is wisdom in order to sort through the opportunities. "Getting wisdom is the most important thing you can do!" wrote Solomon in Proverbs 4:7. Wisdom leads to good judgment, which enables you to make good decisions. And if you're able to make good decisions, you will have the ability to sort through the worthwhile opportunities that will come your way.

How wonderful to be wise,
to be able to analyze and interpret things.
ECCLESIASTES 8:1

GOD'S NEW MATH

You can't outgive God.

You can't apply the rules of mathematics to God. They don't work on Him. In normal arithmetic, if you give something away, you end up with less than you started out with. But in God's math, if you give something to Him, you end up with more than you started out with. It is anti-subtraction. Giving away gives you more.

Now, you might already be thinking about God as an investment scheme. Give money to Him to make more money. (If that worked, you could quit your job and retire on God's annuity program.) But under God's plan, you aren't necessarily going to be paid back in money. What you get in return will be in spiritual blessings. Don't worry about being short-changed. His blessings (in whatever form) are more valuable than what you will be giving.

"I will open the windows of heaven for you.
I will pour out a blessing so great
you won't have enough room to take it in!
Try it! Let me prove it to you!"
MALACHI 3:10

STOP JUDGING

Before you judge someone, examine your own heart.

Have you ever exaggerated the faults of others while excusing or ignoring your own? We all have. That's why the story of the woman caught in adultery has a universal application. What we need to do is put ourselves in the place of "the teachers of religious law" who brought the woman to Jesus. They wanted to see if Jesus would agree that she needed to be stoned.

In what must have been a supremely dramatic moment, Jesus "stooped down and wrote in the dust with his finger" (John 8:6). The teachers demanded an answer, so Jesus stood up and said, "All right, stone her. But let those who have never sinned throw the first stones!" (v. 7). Needless to say, the accusers backed off and "slipped away one by one" (v. 9). The next time we feel compelled to judge someone, we need to remember what Jesus said.

"Let those who have never sinned throw the first stones!"
JOHN 8:7

PURE HEART

*Follow the promptings of your heart rather than
the desires of your flesh.*

The King James Version of the Bible (you know, the one with all the *thee*s and *thou*s) uses the word *flesh* to describe our sinful natures. The Bible says, "Those who are still under the control of their sinful nature [or flesh] can never please God" (Rom. 8:8). The Bible uses the word *heart* to describe the center of our character and will. It doesn't say, "Love the Lord your God will all your flesh," but rather "Love the LORD your God with all your heart" (Deut. 6:5).

When we realize and act upon the fact that Jesus has freed us from a "life that is dominated by sin" (Rom. 7:24), we are free to follow our "heart's desires" (Ps. 37:4). When our hearts are pure, God will fill them with His desires and prompt us to do what He wants us to do, "For God is greater than our hearts" (1 John 3:20).

---

*Take delight in the LORD,
and he will give you your heart's desires.*
PSALM 37:4

INSIDE OUT

The heart produces what the heart receives.

The heart is one of the world's most powerful images. The heart has inspired great poetry *(Search thine own heart)*, philosophy *(The heart has its reasons, which reason does not know)*, catchy song titles ("The Heart Will Go On"), passionate novels *(The Heart Is a Lonely Hunter)*, and profound Scripture *(Blessed are the pure in heart)*. God promises to give you the desires of your heart (Ps. 37:4), as long as your desires are in line with His.

But wait. There's the catch. You don't have a pure heart, and neither do we. As much as we have put the heart on a pedestal, it can be a nasty character. The prophet Jeremiah wrote, "The human heart is most deceitful and desperately wicked" (Jer. 17:9). That's why God asks us to believe in our hearts and invite Him in. He wants to change us from the inside out.

"I, the LORD, search all hearts and examine secret motives."
JEREMIAH 17:10

GOD'S WEB

As you go through the day,
look for opportunities too good to miss.

When you follow the philosophy of *God Is in the Small Stuff*, life becomes much more interesting and exciting. You are alert to God's intricate involvement in the details of your life, and God will never cease to amaze you. God works on many levels every single day of your life. He is present in your casual relationships, prompting you to see others through His eyes of love and compassion. He gives you strength when the pressure mounts at work or at school. God shows Himself through the interactions with those you care about most. As you watch for Him in your circumstances, you begin to see Him in the circumstances of your spouse, your children, and your friends. It's as if God is weaving this huge web composed of the small stuff He is doing in everyone's lives.

Search for the LORD and for his strength,
and keep on searching.
1 CHRONICLES 16:11

WHAT NOT TO LOOK AT

Don't let an inability to overlook the faults of others
be a fault of your own.

Everyone has imperfections (and we aren't talking about facial blemishes). It might be an irritating habit or some other type of personality flaw. We don't all have the same intelligence, and we have different ways of working. So if you are looking for faults in someone else, you are sure to find them. But that is not the approach God wants you to take.

Focusing on the deficiencies of someone else will cause you to think less of that person (and more of yourself). You'll find it hard to cooperate with that person, and you're likely to be critical. God wants you to overlook the faults you see in other people. He wants you to be patient with them and assist them in the areas of their weakness.

Most of us examine other people with a microscope. We would be better off using a mirror.

Be humble and gentle.
Be patient with each other,
making allowance for each other's faults because of your love.
EPHESIANS 4:2

LIVING LETTERS

Hold your relationships tightly, not lightly.

God is very deliberate about the relationships He puts you in. You're going to relate to different people in different ways, but each contact you make with others has a purpose—for you and for them. Don't take your relationships lightly.

What you say—to your family in the morning, your coworkers at the office, the clerk at the grocery store, and the friend on the phone—is important. Your words speak who you are. But don't overemphasize your words at the expense of your life. The truth is that the people you meet are more likely to see Christ in your actions than in your words.

The apostle Paul did a lot of traveling, and he wrote a bunch of letters (they're called *epistles*) to the people he visited. He compared the life of a Christian to a "living letter," meaning that your life is like a "letter of recommendation," written in the hearts of others.

Your lives are a letter written in our hearts,
and everyone can read it and recognize
our good work among you.
2 CORINTHIANS 3:2

READY AND WILLING

Enjoy each day as if it were your last.

Ever since Jesus left the earth nearly two thousand years ago, people have been predicting when the world is going to end. As you may have noticed, no one has gotten it right. Here's our advice on the subject: You need to worry more about the end of your life than the end of the world.

When it comes to the Second Coming of Christ and the end of the world, Jesus said that no one but God knows when it will occur (Matt. 24:36). But when it comes to the end of your life, you know that's going to occur sometime within the next hundred years or so (we're being a little optimistic, but you get the point).

The important thing is to be sure of these two things. Are you ready for the Lord's return? And are you living your life fully each day until Christ comes back or you die, whichever occurs first?

"However, no one knows the day or the hour
when these things will happen."
MATTHEW 24:36

LIFE AFTER DEATH

*People who don't know what happens when they die
don't know that God can give them life.*

Through God's Word, we have confidence and assurance of life after death. Jesus was the prototype of the "resurrected" body that every Christian will someday have in heaven. The old earthly body, with all of its limitations, will be gone. The Christian's new body will be indestructible and immune from all defects.

Jesus gave His followers a glimpse of what was coming when He raised His friend Lazarus from the dead (John 11:17–44). Jesus wanted to demonstrate that physical death isn't the final death. Spiritual death is the only one that counts for eternity.

The same power that Jesus used to transform the dead body of Lazarus is the same power God will use to transform our bodies when Jesus comes back to Earth (1 Cor. 15:51–57).

---

*But let me tell you a wonderful secret God has revealed to us.
Not all of us will die, but we will all be transformed.*
1 CORINTHIANS 15:51

GOD'S GIFT TO YOU

*You don't realize the meaning of Christmas until
you take Jesus out of the manger and put Him in your heart.*

How silly it would be to receive a gift this Christmas and leave it unopened. You would never do that. It might look pretty sitting under the tree, or on a shelf (after the tree has been chopped into kindling), but the decorative value of the package is likely to be minimal compared to the usefulness of the gift itself.

Many people never realize the real meaning of God's Christmas gift—His Son, Jesus. They keep Him wrapped in a religious package, and then set Him on a shelf in their life because He has some decorative value to them. But they never tear away the religious wrappings. They never take Him out of the box and have a real relationship with Him.

Please, don't make the tragic mistake of keeping Jesus under the wrapping. Enjoy the full benefit of Him by getting to know Him personally and intimately.

---

*"The Savior—yes, the Messiah, the Lord—
has been born tonight in Bethlehem, the city of David!"*
LUKE 2:11

THE PUREST OF THE PURE

God will never see holiness in us unless He sees Jesus in us.

We shouldn't be concerned when we come across things in the Bible that puzzle us. God's Word is a book with many layers, kind of like an onion. Some verses are more on the surface and easily understood, while others are deeper and take more time.

The Bible's teaching on holiness is one of those deeper truths. We clearly understand verses that say, "All have sinned" (Rom. 3:23). But when we run across a verse that says, "But now you must be holy in everything you do, just as God—who chose you to be his children—is holy" (1 Pet. 1:15)—well, that's tough to understand. How can sinners be holy?

The only way for us to be holy before God is for God to see Jesus—the purest of the pure—in our lives. Our job isn't to try to be holy, but to let Jesus live through us.

For you know that God paid a ransom to save you. . . .
with the precious lifeblood of Christ, the sinless,
spotless Lamb of God. God chose him for this purpose. . . .
And he did this for you.
1 PETER 1:18–20

REAL HOPE

As a Christian, you have the unique ability to live both now and also in the future.

Do you ever confuse "hope" with "wishing"? When you say, "I hope I get a better job," or "I hope it doesn't rain tomorrow," do you have confidence that what you hope for will actually happen? Or is your hope more like a wish? For the Christian, hoping is believing. We put our hope in God, that what He says in His Word is true. And we put our hope in Jesus, that what He did on the cross counts for us now and for the future.

We can believe by faith that Jesus lives in us here on Earth, and we can look forward with complete confidence that Jesus is coming again to take us to heaven. This is not wishing hope. This is real hope, the kind that enables us to live for God now while we look forward to living with Him in the future.

We should live in this evil world with self-control,
right conduct, and devotion to God,
while we look forward to that wonderful event when the glory of
our great God and Savior, Jesus Christ, will be revealed.
TITUS 2:12–13

OBEDIENCE MATTERS

Living a life that pleases God doesn't come automatically.

Living life so God sees Jesus in us requires something of us: obedience. Accepting Jesus and what He did for us on the cross puts us in God's good graces (after all, we are saved by His grace), but it doesn't automatically mean we're going to live our lives the way God wants us to. God didn't force you to accept Jesus, and He's not going to force you to live like Jesus. But He is asking.

More than anything else, God wants us to imitate Jesus in our lives. He wants us to look at each situation we encounter and ask the question, "What would Jesus do?" Professor Dallas Willard put it this way: "Live your life the way Jesus would live your life if He had your life to live." The best way we know to do that is to know what Jesus said and did, and then go out and do it.

Follow God's example in everything you do,
because you are his dear children.
Live a life filled with love for others,
following the example of Christ, who loved you
and gave himself as a sacrifice to take away your sins.
EPHESIANS 5:1–2

When God's Patience Runs Out

It's never a good idea to play the percentages with God,
because God is right 100 percent of the time.

We think we know why God is the only One Who knows when the world is going to end. He hasn't set the date yet. The Bible says, "The Lord isn't really being slow about his promise to return, as some people think. No, he is being patient for your sake" (2 Pet. 3:9).

When you have patience, you wait for the right moment. We believe that God is waiting for the right moment to send Jesus back to Earth (ending the world as we know it). And that moment has a lot to do with people giving God their hearts. Of course, even God's patience is going to run out at some point, which begs the question: Why would anyone want to take a chance of being on the wrong side of God's patience?

That is why the LORD says,
"Turn to me now, while there is time! Give me your hearts."
JOEL 2:12

THE SECOND COMING

Jesus came to Earth in the past,
and He is coming again in the future.
Thank God for the first coming and get ready for the Second.

The New Testament begins with the historical record of the first coming of Jesus to Earth, when God became a human and lived on Earth for a while. (One of the names of Jesus, *Immanuel*, means "God with us.") The Bible ends with the fact that Jesus, God in the flesh, will return someday. Jesus came as a Savior the first time (the name *Jesus* means "Savior"). When He comes again, He will be coming to reward and repay according to what people have done. And He will come unexpectedly.

All those who have accepted God's plan of salvation through Jesus will receive the wonderful reward of eternal life in heaven. Those who have refused will receive the judgment they deserve. Are you ready for the "soon" return of Jesus?

"Yes, I am coming soon!"
REVELATION 22:20

TAKE A GOOD LOOK

When you see God in the small stuff,
your life becomes more meaningful.

We like to compare seeing God in the small stuff to looking at the stars. If you've never studied astronomy, you could look at the stars all night long and never know anything about them. The sight would be beautiful, but your appreciation would be limited. However, if you were to do a little study, get a star chart, and plunk yourself down with a telescope, those little points of light would take on much more meaning and significance.

It's the same with the small points of light in your life—the places where God is working. If you don't make an effort to know God, if you don't read the Bible regularly, if you don't try to look at your circumstances more closely, you'll miss out on the amazing things God is doing now and wants to do in the future.

May grace and peace be yours from God our Father
and from the Lord Jesus Christ.
GALATIANS 1:3

SCRIPTURE REFERENCE INDEX

TOPICAL REFERENCE INDEX

ABOUT THE AUTHORS

BRUCE BICKEL was a frustrated comedian. (He was frustrated because he wasn't very funny.) So he pursued a career as a court jester: He became a lawyer. He lives in Fresno, California, with his wife, Cheryl. Bruce is on the Board of Trustees at Westmont College, where their children, Lindsey and Matt, have attended.

STAN JANTZ has worked in Christian retail for more than twenty-five years. He and his son, Scott, build and maintain Web sites for businesses and Christian organizations. Stan lives in Fresno with his wife, Karin, and he serves on the Board of Trustees at Biola University, where their children, Hillary and Scott, have attended.

BRUCE AND STAN spend their free time as cultural observers. They sit back and observe society. (They don't like hobbies where they have to sweat.) They have written twenty books.

The guys would love to hear from you. Send them an E-mail at:

guide@bruceandstan.com

or write to them the old-fashioned way at:

BRUCE AND STAN
P.O. Box 25565
Fresno, CA 93729

You can also follow the continuing adventures of Bruce and Stan on the Internet at:

www.bruceandstan.com